DR GILBERT CHILDS attended the Steiner teacher training course at Michael Hall in East Sussex after war service. He later studied at four universities, with his doctoral thesis entitled 'Steiner Education as Historical Necessity'. After teaching at State and Steiner schools he spent twenty years as a tutor in a further education college for severely physically disabled students. He is, in retirement, a full-time author and keen gardener. His published works include *Your Reincarnating Child* and *Truth, Beauty and Goodness*.

Understand Your Temperament!

A guide to the four temperaments:
CHOLERIC, SANGUINE, PHLEGMATIC, MELANCHOLIC

Dr Gilbert Childs

Sophia Books

Sophia Books
Hillside House, The Square
Forest Row, RH18 5ES

www.rudolfsteinerpress.com

Published by Sophia Books 2009
An imprint of Rudolf Steiner Press

First published in 1995 and reprinted in 1998 and 2004

The publishers gratefully acknowledge permission to reproduce
illustrations from *The Structure of Human Personality* by H.J.
Eysenck, Methuen & Co., 1970

A catalogue record for this book is available from the
British Library

ISBN 978 1 85584 025 6

Cover by Andrew Morgan Design
Typeset by Imprint Publicity Service, Crawley Down, Sussex
Printed and bound in Great Britain by Cromwell Press Group Limited,
Trowbridge, Wiltshire

Know then thyself, presume not God to scan;
The proper study of mankind is man.
Alexander Pope
An Essay on Man (1733)

There is indeed an intermediary between what is brought over from earlier lives on Earth and what is provided by heredity. This intermediary has the more universal qualities provided by family, nation and race, but is at the same time capable of individualization. That which stands midway between the line of heredity and the individuality is expressed in the word temperament.

Rudolf Steiner

Contents

1. The Same – only Different!

The Irish say that everyone is the same, only different. This difference is due mainly to the fact that every individual has a different *temperament*. You will be able to classify everyone's main temperament with confidence and accuracy after you have read this book. So what temperament are you? How important is it to know what your temperament is, and those of your family, your workmates, your colleagues? If you want to know how a person is likely to react in a given set of circumstances, then you should know what their temperament is. So if you want to know the secrets of your own psychological make-up, and also those of other people's – and who doesn't? – then this book is for you. You can only benefit, because there have to be advantages all round. The self-knowledge you will gain will bring greater understanding of your worst enemy as well as your dearest friend.

Very often we can see behaviour patterns in our friends and acquaintances that remain consistent. These patterns are usually so constant that you may well be able to predict how they would react in certain situations or circumstances. How often do you find yourself saying something like: "Well, I knew you would do that!" You are able to recognize at once whether Susan or Jim *is acting out of character*. "It's not like Bill to do that," you will say, "I can't understand it."

When you find yourself saying this kind of thing, it makes you think whether you have misjudged this person after all. You start asking yourself whether even

1

you know what kind of person your best friend really is. You have doubtless heard people – probably divorced, separated, or who have broken a steady partnership – say, "I've lived with him/her for five years, and didn't really know them – what they were really like." When we begin to lose our ability to judge other people's characters, we start to lose faith in ourselves as well, and wonder whether we are everything we thought we were! And that can come as something of a shock to us, as if reality is not what we thought it was.

The difference between personality and character

We all know that "there's nowt so strange as folk", and that "people are funnier than anybody", but there is no need to imagine that you will *never* get to understand people as they really are. You will certainly know some individuals who let people "walk all over" them, and others who get into a temper over the slightest thing. You will probably have thought about these various *types* of people, and how they fall into certain general categories, such as quick-tempered, easy-going, the "never-happy-unless-they're-miserable" sorts, those who are "on the go" all the time, and so on.

   People's *personalities* show in their individual differences. They reveal their philosophy of life in their actions, their outlook on the world, and in their views and opinions on various issues. It is what helps to make people different in their ideas, beliefs, education and upbringing and so on. We all have our various *characteristics* in the way of temperament dealt out to us at our birth like so many cards from a pack. These basic tendencies and qualities constitute the foundation upon which we build our lives, from early childhood to old age. But what matters in the long run is *how we play* these cards, how our individuality makes use of them. It is by our behaviour, by what we actually *do* that we express our personality.

Our *character*, on the other hand, helps us when we look for habitual behaviour. It may be said with considerable justification that every deed we do, every act we perform, just how we behave in whatever situation or circumstance is *always in response to some need* that we have at the time. This need may be prompted by what we feel, what we think, what simply has to be done in the sense of duty. Usually, every action prompts a reaction, and it is the nature of this reaction or response that so often reflects our temperament. In other words, we reveal our inner selves, our real selves, our character – what we actually are as human beings. The word *character* in this context means rather what imparts *characteristics*, and whether a certain individual's life-style is one of utter respectability on the one hand, or one of criminal tendencies on the other, is of no significance.

It has been known for centuries that people really do fall into certain categories or 'types' on the very grounds of consistent patterns of behaviour and attitudes towards other people and life in general. These patterns will be in the nature of *habit*; in other words, those in which a person usually reacts to a given situation. It would be odd, for example, if an easy-going individual, well-known for this characteristic, suddenly adopted loud, aggressive behaviour, shouting and laying down the law to everyone. So we would be justified in thinking that the ways in which we usually behave are, as it were, built right into our very constitution. Assuming this to be so, it would be reasonable to suppose that the consistency of people's behaviour shows in their actual outward physical appearance, and as we shall see, this is actually the case.

What are the four temperaments?

The *characteristics* which are typical of human behaviour fall into four main groups, and these are represented by the *four temperaments*. These, according to custom, go back in history as far as the Ancient Greeks, who associated the *four elements*, namely Fire, Air, Water and Earth, with the four temperaments, and the following table will help to make matters clear. Medieval physicians claimed associations with our physical constitutions, which corresponded also with the 'four humours', and which they thought gave us our basic temperamental moods:

Temperament	Element	Humours
Choleric	Fire	Yellow bile
Sanguine	Air	Blood
Phlegmatic	Water	Body fluids
Melancholic	Earth	Black bile

Please do not be alarmed by the following dictionary definitions: [1] Choleric (bad-tempered, passionate and irascible); [2] Sanguine (cheerful, confident and optimistic); [3] Phlegmatic (stolid, unemotional, unexcitable), and [4] Melancholic (dejected, pensive, depressed). These brief dictionary meanings of the terms in themselves give only a sketchy idea as to why people are put into categories according to such definitive characteristics. In any case, they are but a tiny fraction of the numbers of other attributes which are also applicable, as we shall see.

Many people object to this admittedly rough and ready manner of sorting people out according to their general personal qualities, attributes and traits of character, calling it unscientific and difficult to prove. If you are one of these, then I hope that you will postpone your final verdict until you have read this book to the last page. That which satisfies the laws of science must be seen to *work*, and match theory with practice. The doctrine of the four temperaments has stood the test of time, and will be seen to do just this. William Shakespeare, in his play *Julius Caesar*, characterizes the phlegmatic and melancholic very neatly:

> Let me have men about me that are fat;
> Sleek-headed men and such as sleep o' nights.
> Yond Cassius has a lean and hungry look;
> He thinks too much; such men are dangerous.
> Act I, Scene II

Among famous composers, whose musical style as well as general appearance give ample indication of their main temperament are: Beethoven (choleric); Mozart (sanguine); Bruckner (phlegmatic), and Chopin (melancholic).

Four into three will not go!

Modern psychology places great emphasis on the *differences* in individual behaviour, whilst in the categorizing of people by reference to the notion of the temperaments, stress is placed on their *similarities*. So we shall be able to agree that the Irish are right after all, odd as it may seem. We really are all in very many ways the same, but nevertheless different. If we weren't, we should not only find the world a very dull place, but we shouldn't be able to understand one another either! And it is very interesting, even fascinating, to determine just how different we are, and how much the same.

When discussing the various temperaments, psychologists always make much ado about people's *physiognomy*, that is to say, their stature, build and other physical characteristics. Usually, these are described as *endomorphic* (well-rounded and heavy), *ectomorphic* (tall and lightly built), and *mesomorphic* (robust and muscular); but again, these portrayals tell us only a very little part of the whole story. In any case, this typology is very suspect, and the issues involved will be discussed in detail in later chapters.

It is generally agreed that there are, by tradition, *four* temperaments. Modern science seems to persist in the view that there are *three* types of physical build and stature. Now, as we all know, according to the rules of simple arithmetic, four into three will not 'go' – unless we end up with a very messy fraction not representative of very much in real-life terms. So what is the answer to this apparent contradiction?

Ordinary observation of our fellow human beings tells us that there are – *basically* – only *two* sorts of people: those who are tall and thin, and those who are short and fat. However, I am hoping to convince you that there are *two kinds* of each of these *two types*, making *four* physical categories. As a rough guide, melancholics are tall and wiry, with long faces; sanguines are generally not quite so tall, but lightly built and with oval or heart-shaped faces; phlegmatics are rather short by comparison, and usually well-upholstered, with chubby features; the cholerics are also short but more stocky, more muscular, square-shouldered and with regular features. These are merely preliminary indications; I shall go into particulars later, when I discuss each temperament in detail.

There are basic similarities and polarities among the four temperaments, and it is helpful to bear these in mind. The two introverted types are obviously the melancholics and phlegmatics, and the sanguines and cholerics are clearly mainly extrovert. Polarities are readily detectable between melancholics and sanguines on the one hand, and phlegmatics and cholerics on the other. Very often just these polarities show up in people, and a more balanced character results. At the same time, however, it is invariably the case that one temperament predominates; and this is why it is always best to carry out your observations over a fairly long period of time before determining which one this is. The acid test is always your ability to predict correctly a person's reactions to a given situation, or in a particular set of circumstances. Temperaments are always consistent in their basic nature, and dependable in revealing the patterns of people's actions and reactions. This must be so, for they are actually built into our very physical constitution, and there for all to see!

These polarities reveal themselves in the following chart, which deals with the strength or otherwise of the arousal of an individual, and that person's span and intensity of attention, and how strongly this is maintained.

MELANCHOLIC
Attention not easily aroused,
strongly persevering

PHLEGMATIC
Attention least easily aroused,
strongly persevering

CHOLERIC
Attention most easily aroused,
most strongly persevering

SANGUINE
Attention easily aroused,
little strength of perseverance

This is a very helpful guide to determining an individual's behaviour in the respects referred to, for they provide reliable clues to their temperament even after a few minutes' conversation.

Which temperament is the best?

It cannot be claimed that any one temperament is in some way better than any of the others. They all have their good points, and also those which are less desirable, as will become clear as we go along. In fact, we all possess all four temperaments, but in unequal proportions; and this is of course why we are indeed all the same, but different! It is invariably the case that each one of us shows characteristic behaviour traits of *two* temperaments, though there is usually one that predominates, and is recognizable for the most part in our actual body build. This is mainly responsible for our primary features, our 'natural' disposition, and it is very rare for an individual to behave in the unbalanced way that would result from possessing one temperament only. As a rule, there are traces of a third in some degree, whilst the fourth is for the most part overpowered by the other three, particularly the two main ones.

It is very interesting to observe the finer points of a person's appearance which are so important in deciding their main temperament. I shall discuss these matters of detail when I deal with each one, and I shall be very surprised if you don't find people even more fascinating than you did before. It is easy to study people's behaviour because it is so interesting, and often quite amusing if you find one or two who show the very same character traits and body build as you yourself do! You will never again be bored whilst standing in a queue, travelling by bus or train, or waiting around in an airport lounge! There is also a bonus in all this, as you will soon be able to understand your colleagues – not to mention friends and acquaintances – at greater depth.

So you think you know yourself, and others, maybe better even than they know themselves? Well, life is full of surprises, and so is this book. In it you will find some answers to problems endemic in people's lives – at home, in the workplace and in all areas of social interaction with other human beings.

A pause for reflection

This book contains information about the inner workings of people's feelings and reasonings about many concerns in life. You can find out why some people over-react *SO* quickly to what has been said to them, and why some people seem reluctant to react at all and are so irritating at times. You will know why, before you have even finished this book, your friend who has been such a misery at times is quite happy being miserable, and that others who get on especially well with everyone, do so because of their temperament.

Once you have read and understood this book you will find people more interesting, indeed more fascinating, and will become, I believe, more tolerant of your own shortcomings and more tolerant of others' strange ways.

Let's face it. Number one always comes first, and that goes for all of us. We are more interested in ourselves than in anyone else because it's only natural. What's more, we think we know ourselves better than anyone else does – but in that we could be wrong!

Otherwise, why do other people have to sort us out now and again? Why can't we always do it ourselves? This is the age of the *counsellor* – the person who knows better than you what your problems are. We all think that we are private people, and why should we make what we really feel, and what we really think, public to anyone except to those whom we choose?

The sad truth is that we *don't* always know ourselves, or see ourselves, as we really are, and other people can very often observe this in our behaviour. Of course, you can see them as they can't see themselves, so it works both ways. As Robert Burns, the canny Scots poet, in his poem 'To a Louse' put it:

> "Oh wad some Power the giftie gie us
> To see oursels as ithers see us.
> It wad frae mony a blunder free us,
>   And foolish notion."

Of course, the trouble is that we don't want to run the risk of telling our best friend the naked truth about themselves; otherwise it could be the end of (yet another!) beautiful friendship.

2. The Psychology of the Temperaments

Generally speaking, the notion of the four temperaments is regarded with a fair degree of suspicion by
academic psychologists of orthodox persuasion. They
regard it as not being 'scientific' enough, as it is based
on apparently loosely accepted generalizations which
are difficult to prove. However, as we have seen, the
doctrine of the four temperaments has been around
for more than two thousand years, and so can claim to
have stood the test of time. If they disregard it, that is
their loss; and if it is not 'scientific', then common
sense applied to careful observation is not scientific
either. I discuss the so-called Hypothesis of
Embryological Development in Appendix II. I am
sure that you will then be able more easily to discern
what makes sense, and what, if anything, does not!

Introverts and extroverts

By long tradition people have been classified into those
who, in general terms, may be *introverted* in their usual
patterns of behaviour and attributes, and those who
tend to be *extroverted*. We do not need to be a psycholo-
gist to understand this – everyday experience shows
this, and common sense confirms it to be the case. We
live in two worlds: the outer world which is in every
sense public, and which we all share with everyone else,
and our own private inner world, to which no-one has
access unless we choose.

Obviously, therefore, introverts tend to be preoccupied with their inner thoughts and feelings. For this

reason such people are often referred to as being mainly *reflective* in their general behaviour. They appear for the most part passive, but this trait is generally confined to the outer world. However. they are certainly active in their inner world of thoughts and feelings, hopes and fears, ambitions and disappointments. They tend to turn things over in their minds a great deal, are cautious in their ways, and habitually act with forethought and due consideration. Such people often keep themselves to themselves, and you would never find them the 'life and soul' of any party or rave-up!

Extroverts, on the other hand, are just the people for this kind of role. They are considered to be the *active* types, those who find their fulfilment in the hurly-burly of life, and who enjoy other people's company more than their own, perhaps. They tend to be constantly 'on the go', and find their enjoyment in doing things or watching others doing things – playing football or cricket, for example. You would seldom find them, book in hand, sunk deep into an armchair, oblivious to what is going on around them! Reacting to a situation swiftly and often impulsively, they barely stop to think – they must be where the action is! Already, then, we can construct a simple model, one of several that will get more and more complex and informative as we proceed:

Introverts (reflective)   –   Phlegmatics and Melancholics
Extroverts (active)   –   Cholerics and Sanguines

Convergent and divergent thinkers

Now, as well as this kind of classification there is another. Those individuals whose powers of concentration are good, and whose memories are retentive and reliable, belong to the *convergent* type of thinker. They find it comparatively easy to handle abstract ideas, and are usually methodical and thorough in their work habits. In general, it may be said that people in this category, although not necessarily anti-social in their attitudes and behaviour, nevertheless often prefer to occupy themselves with *things* or objects rather than other human beings.

It is not surprising that convergent thinkers are good at problem-solving, for it is their habit to think logically. They are inclined to be conventional and orthodox in their attitudes, and inclined to be rather authoritarian, and fixed and rigid in their ways of thinking, feeling and doing. Many follow careers which do not bring them into contact with other people; and white-coated scientists working away in the isolation of their laboratory are a fairly close stereotype of this. They tend to put up barriers around themselves, where they feel safe and secure, and then hide behind them. As a rule, their range of interests is comparatively narrow, and are the type which calls for precision of thought and action. This kind of impersonal attitude and shunning of inter-personal interaction tends to leave them emotionally under-developed, for they are commonly shy of revealing their true feelings.

On the other hand, *divergent* thinkers often find that their thoughts, so to speak, run away with them, and they often find it difficult to concentrate on the job in hand. This being so, they may find facts and figures difficult to remember, owing to a tendency to be some-what scatter-brained. They are inclined to be artistic, with powers of vivid imagination, and are quick to find solutions to any problems that come their way, very often relying on their intuition rather than reasoning powers. Divergent thinkers frequently possess keen social consciences, and much prefer to be with their fellow human beings rather than inanimate objects. It might fairly be said that whereas divergent thinkers take refuge in things from people, convergents take refuge from people in things!

Divergents, being for the most part *active*, take little trouble to hide their feelings – or opinions for that matter – and their wide range of interests ensures that they accumulate general knowledge at a rapid rate. Unfortunately, they frequently find it difficult to remember much of what they have learned! They are more flexible in their attitudes than convergents, and are more willing to compromise. Their creative powers are frequently considerable, and they are also inclined to be unconventional and unorthodox in their views, and even their lifestyle.

There are no appreciable differences in the range of intelligence between these two groups, though it must be said that convergent thinkers, with their more efficient memories, tend to do better at written examinations, particularly those containing questions of a 'closed' nature. Divergent thinkers, on the other hand, do better at 'open-ended' questions and at those of a multiple-choice nature.

It is therefore reasonable to classify the two types in terms of basic temperament:

Divergent thinkers   –   Cholerics and Sanguines
Convergent thinkers   –   Phlegmatics and Melancholics

Thus we may say that, in the majority of cases, introverted people are either basically phlegmatic or melancholic, and likely to be convergent thinkers, whereas extroverted individuals are usually classifiable as either choleric or sanguine *in temperament*, and tend towards divergent habits of thinking. From our brief examination of the main characteristics that are readily observable in people's behaviour, such categorization makes sense.

The stable and unstable temperaments

It can be claimed with some justification that most people, in terms of habitual behaviour, can be classified as being more stable in temperament, whilst others tend towards instability. In other words, there are those people who are rather more *consistent* in their patterns of behaviour, and those who are less predictable in this respect, and these correspond in their main characteristics also to temperamental categories, as follows:

Stable temperaments   –   Phlegmatics and Sanguines
Unstable temperaments   –   Cholerics and Melancholics

It may seem strange that the stolid, reliable, even-tempered and passive phlegmatics should be associated with the flighty, unreliable, lively and nervous sanguines in this way. But these patterns for the most part remain constant. Phlegmatic people are generally so engrossed in their own inner world that they take little notice of what is going on around them – they simply can't be bothered. Objects in themselves hold little interest for them – unless of course they are edible objects! Sanguine people show stability in that their behaviour patterns are also consistent, in spite of the fact that *inconsistency* is very much a part of these!

They find it quite natural to be superficial, impressionable, sociable and impulsive, for these attributes in themselves are sanguine in their very essence. So sanguines and phlegmatics are stable inasmuch as their behaviour patterns remain extremely consistent. At the same time their respective characteristics are seen to be polar opposites!

The main temperamental characteristics

We are now in a position of being able to form basic models of behavioural attitudes of the vast majority of ordinary people in their more complex form. Everyday life experience teaches us that things are not rigidly compartmentalized, and so it is with the temperaments. But as we proceed, you will see that your own experiences will confirm that their fundamental rationale is in the main valid and reliable.

These characteristics being what they are, in terms of *behavioural difficulties*, the table below represents our findings so far:

Personality	{ Melancholics	–	Unstable introverts
Difficulties	{ Phlegmatics	–	Stable introverts
Behavioural	{ Cholerics	–	Unstable extroverts
Difficulties	{ Sanguines	–	Stable extroverts

It can be readily understood that melancholics and phlegmatics, being both inclined to introversion and convergent thinking, will exhibit personality difficulties associated with a strong inner life. They are inwardly turned, concerned rather with themselves and their own world rather than other people's worlds. As a general rule, their problems and troubles are often self-induced by very reason of their psychological orientation, which is towards themselves rather than towards the outside world. Phlegmatic people are seen to be unduly concerned, even preoccupied, with their sense of inner well-being, their bodily comforts, including of course what they eat and drink! They are representative of the 'fat and jolly' stereotype, good-humoured, placid and even-tempered. Melancholic folk are never really happy unless they are, by other people's standards at any rate, miserable. Their stereotype is that of 'Job's comforter', ever ready to place their own 'misery' at the disposal of others who are genuinely distressed or upset! So if you find a phlegmatic who is really unhinged, or a melancholic suffering from pathological melancholia, you find real personality problems.

Conversely, it is the cholerics and sanguines, whose attentions are claimed by the outer world and social interaction, who are more likely to be involved in problems and difficulties associated with outer behaviour. It is to be expected that quick-tempered, irritable and swiftly-reacting aggressive cholerics will be involved in conflicts and disagreements of all kinds, fighting always to overcome whatever adversary, real or imagined. In a manner of speaking, they are by their very nature walking disasters that are waiting to happen. Sanguine people could be regarded as instability personified, ever poking their noses into everything, curious about everything and everybody, never being able to find peace or satisfaction. For them, the grass is always greener in somebody else's patch, and they are ever restless for satisfaction, which ever eludes them. So you can imagine for yourself just what trouble they can make for themselves!

The temperaments in their polarities

In many respects our very weaknesses are our strengths, and our unmistakable strengths our weaknesses. Virtue taken to excess very often manifests as vice, and every situation, state, circumstance and condition carries within it, so to speak, the seeds of its own destruction. So it is with our particular sets of temperamental propensities.

It is clear that the nature of our temperament characteristics arrange themselves as two pairs of polar opposites. Our next step is to collate these, and this is best done by means of another fourfold arrangement – the quadrant.

Figure 1

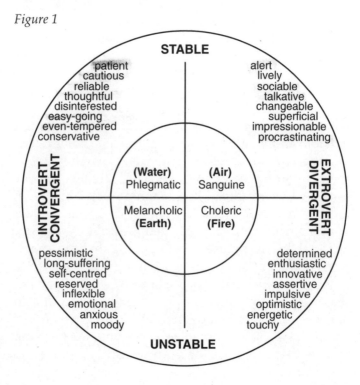

I have included the so-called Four Elements of Ancient Greek science because they are useful indicators of the very basics of the temperaments with which they are associated. This arrangement goes back at least as far as Galen (130?–?200), the Greek physician and writer, if not well before.

Melancholic people give the impression of being heavily weighed down, physically as well as mentally. It is as if they are carrying the world, with all its troubles and woes, on their shoulders, and in a sense this is what they actually feel. They feel under the influence in all its aspects of *gravity*, and this is an attribute of the very earth itself. They give the impression of being over-wrought, over-downcast, and overburdened, overwhelmed by the smallest of life's troubles. Every molehill is a mountain, every ditch an abyss – heaven has fallen and earth has collapsed!

The phlegmatics, as well as living mainly in their body fluids, are readily associated with the element of Water in many other ways. Water always seeks to find its own level, and the even-temperedness of this temperament is reflected in this characteristic. However, just as there can be violent ocean storms, phlegmatic people, once their extraordinarily high levels of tolerance are breached, are capable of more violent behaviour than any normal choleric. But they seem to remain for the most part slow, dull, sluggish and apathetic, skulking idly around, lethargic, listless and languid, too lazy to get out of their own way, not to mention other people's, and in danger of becoming so mindless as to drive other people out of their own minds, and – well, anything can happen after that!

The fiery nature exhibited in all cholerics is legendary, and needs little amplification. All the heat, if not light, is there, but even when the fire dies down and turns to ashes, the choleric person will, like the phoenix, rise again from them, once more to sally forth in search of – if not fame and fortune – then the next challenge or obstacle to overcome. Choleric individuals, hell-bent on getting on with whatever job needs to be done at the time, often at the expense of practically any other consideration, find it becoming their overwhelming compulsion, preoccupation, or even obsession. Such typical 'workaholics' are known to all of us, who by their one-track-minded approach to things, run the risk of ruining their own lives as well as those of their family.

The sanguine temperament is rightly associated with the element of Air, for it is in essence just like the wind, endlessly coming and going, hither and thither, "blowing where it listeth". Sanguine people can often be accused with some justification of being 'airy-fairy' in their ways and attitudes. They are ever ready to pass on from one passing interest to the next, restless and ever-changing, just like the wind itself.

Excessively sanguine people are scatterbrained and changeable, who dissipate their energies on trivialities, unable to concentrate their thoughts and actions on a single thing, racing around so fast that their feet don't touch the ground, and who eventually exhaust those close to them as well as themselves, so that they are all in danger of having nervous breakdowns!

There is much wisdom buried in these symbols of the basic Elements of Fire, Air, Water and Earth, and the figure at the top of page 21 is well worth pondering.

The physiognomy of the four typical temperament types has been touched on only briefly so far, but they will be described in detail in the following chapters. These also deal with the appropriate personal

Unstable

(Earth)	(Fire)
Personality problems	Behavioural problems
MELANCHOLIC	CHOLERIC

{   Introvert   Extrovert }
{
{   Reflective   Active }

PHLEGMATIC	SANGUINE
Personality problems	Behavioural problems
(Water)	(Air)

Stable

characteristics feature by feature, so that a comprehensive portrait of each temperament will gradually emerge. Caricatures of them may be helpful at this stage:

Figure 2

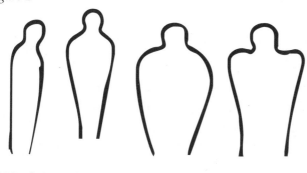

Melancholic   Sanguine   Phlegmatic   Choleric

Children and their temperaments

Needless to say, we all arrive in the world with our temperaments already determined, as I shall consistently demonstrate. Heredity alone cannot account for *all* the characteristics we are born with, because different members of the same family vary in their qualities and attributes. We are, each one of us, unique as individuals; the number of possible permutations of temperamental characteristics must be incalculable. Everyone in the world shares the same universal qualities which go to make up the character and personality of each single individual; for were it not so, we would not be able to understand one another nor communicate with one another.

It is important to remember that *all* children up to the age of ten or eleven can be expected to show typical characteristics associated with the *sanguine* temperament. Whatever their main temperament is, or their secondary one, they will be, as it were, overlaid by a pattern of sanguine traits. Ordinary observation shows this to be so. What healthy child is not inclined to be active and energetic, inquisitive, curious, adventurous, interested – for a time – in everything that is going on around them? With their fertile imagination and natural urge to express themselves in all kinds of creatively artistic ways, however crude they may be; with their bubbling enthusiasms and constantly changing moods, their free, uninhibited and unselfconscious behaviour, do not older folk envy them?

Of course, we also see among a gathering of children the usual boisterous, aggressive, quarrelsome cholerics; the flighty, volatile, mercurial sanguines; the stolid, stodgy, disinterested – until meal-times, that is – phlegmatics, and the quiet, reserved, retiring melancholics. But now and again, say at a party, picnic or outing, or at the leisure centre or recreation grounds, sanguine characteristics will shine through, as well we all know. All the sociableness, spontaneousness and inherently amiable characteristics so clearly seen in all sanguines are invariably present in every child, and this is what makes them so charming.

Perhaps the most important thing of all to remember is that no-one should *on any account* attempt to change the temperament your child already possesses. If you do try, you will only succeed in confusing and bewildering the child. Their temperament is built into their very constitution, and any attempt to change it would be equal to resorting to plastic surgery if you think that their nose is too long, or even if their legs are too long! You must learn to understand their temperament and go along with it; for only by this means will they grow up without running the risk of psychological damage.

If your child is a choleric, remember that by very reason of their temperament they are looking – not so much for trouble, perhaps – but certainly for challenges to meet, obstacles to overcome, and situations where they can be active, preferably to some useful purpose. Always give them tasks to do that are just beyond their capabilities at their particular stage of development, at the same time remaining alert to the possibility that you may have misjudged the difficulty or magnitude of such jobs, and be instantly ready to give help in such circumstances. Never forget that children are more often than not 'naughty' simply because they are bored. So make sure that there is something for them to *do*, for it is being involved in *activities* that enables co-ordination between eye and limb to develop, manual skills to improve, and all-round motor development to be enhanced.

However, it is by assigning tasks that are appropriate in most respects that you will ensure that their powers of determination, perseverance, resolution and will-power will develop in a healthy way. I need hardly add that no attempt must be made to 'break' such a child's will. Ordinary childish wilfulness can be wearing and wearying, but the best thing to do in face of such behaviour is to resort to the well-tried ploys of distracting their attention, or joining in what they are doing. Obviously, any kind of belittling attitude towards, or thoughtless criticism of children's work or attempts at performing any task is very much out of order: praise is always preferable to blame, as a positive attitude is to a negative one. Always a good thing to do when dealing with choleric children is to demonstrate to them some skill or expertise for which they will admire and look up to you. Show them just how clever you are, and it will inspire them; tell them that when they are grown up then they will be able to do what you are doing now, and it will fire them with the determination to succeed.

In the case of sanguine children, who may drive you to distraction with their endless interruptions, questions and demands, and who can never settle down to do anything for longer than a few minutes before coming to plead that they are bored, the answer is to be relentless in your search for some activity or other that *will* attract their attention and maintain it for a reasonable length of time. This means closely monitoring them in their involvement with a seemingly endless stream of interests, activities, pastimes, hobbies, games and so on, until one day you may discover just what does actually grab their attention and keep it. Try to present them with varied interests, which will grow and expand. For example, if their latest passion and consuming interest is flowers, take them to visit the local community gardens and parks, or even those of the nearest stately homes. A visit to a flower festival in your local church, or even an ordinary village flower show, might well prove to be the very occasion which kindles a life-long interest in flowers, gardening, or flower-arranging, and which will provide a kind of much-needed 'anchor' or focus of attention – or even a career.

Make sure, too, that they meet many other children and grown-ups, because they are naturally amiable and sociable, and will be seeking an individual to whom they will feel they can attach themselves. They spread themselves around in so many directions and engage in so many activities that they will find relief if they can, so to speak, find rest and contentment in the company of one personality whom they can grow to love or even revere. This may be a sympathetic, tolerant individual, possibly of mature years, to whom they can relate. Again, do not grouse or grumble at their restlessness and inevitable disappointments and dissatisfactions, and even if they do try your patience at times, search your own heart for even a tiny trace of melancholy that must surely be there somewhere – and indulge in a little martyrdom!

Phlegmatic children may well present themselves as well-behaved, compliant and tractable, and to be relied on to do as they are told most of the time. Their lives are likely to be divided between the kitchen table and the local sweetshop, but do try not to bribe them too often! They are not, as a rule, especially interested in having many friends and acquaintances, or even toys and gadgets. You will find it very difficult to try actually to *instil* a particular interest, maybe that of one of their siblings, or perhaps even one of your own, if a glimmer of it does not already exist. Do not expect anything in the nature of enthusiasm, eagerness or zeal; just be satisfied if those eyes with their customary faraway look light up with the tiniest spark of curiosity!

The strategy to adopt is to introduce them to other children of their own age who already have hobbies, interests or pursuits that they are willing to share. The more expertise and accomplishment that such acquaintances can show, especially if the interest is deep, the better, particularly if they are not too excitable or boisterous, and can show patience and forbearance. Remember that phlegmatics are not in general particularly interested in people, so watch for opportunities to foster the slightest inclination in that direction.

Children who are sadly aware, even at a tender age, of the sorrow and grief in the world around them, are of course those with the melancholic as their main temperament. If they haven't got any immediate problems they will certainly create them, so on no account try to jolly them along, attempt to cheer them up or make their miserable lives happy, for they will have none of it. Their natural inclination is to shut themselves up inside themselves, and this tendency should to a reasonable extent be respected. Don't forget that unhappiness and gloom is part of their world, and that they are entitled to be allowed to live in it.

As melancholics are familiar with pain and suffering, real or imagined, they understand it. The way to cheer a melancholic child up is to sit down next to them and pour out the most woeful, tragic and pitiful story you can think up, in the most mournfully low and dejected tones you can muster. Their interest will be stirred at once; but if the tale you recount is a true one, so much the better. Make sure that the wretchedness and misery of the hero, heroine or perhaps an animal is dwelt upon at lingering length, sparing your listener only a few of the most gory details. Disasters and catastrophes should be your stock-in-trade in all this, with calamity, affliction and misfortune appearing at every turn of the story. If this kind of misery can be experienced in such vicarious fashion, there is every likelihood of melancholic children growing up with a fuller appreciation of the wretchedness that afflicts other people in the world, and may well inspire them to do something about it when they are adult. Such as these are society's born voluntary workers, charity helpers, relief carers and suchlike – genuine friends in need.

Growing older with your temperament

Generally speaking, it becomes easier and easier to determine a person's temperament from their bodily stature as they get older. Choleric people keep their figures as a rule, for they tend to remain active and burn up those excess calories. Sanguines too generally retain their regular build, but with the standard concessions to that 'spare tyre' and facial lines. Phlegmatics will almost certainly put on weight, very often in spite of a few half-hearted efforts to retain their rounded charms. Melancholics tend to become even more wiry and spare, and their already lean features more lined and wrinkled. So not only do the basic physical characteristics become more pronounced and so more discernible, but as a rule the patterns of people's habitual behaviour reveal themselves more clearly and consistently.

All children, right up to the stage of adolescence, despite their basic temperament, show unmistakable signs of it being overlaid, as it were, by *sanguine* characteristics, and this is readily observed by their lively movements and demeanour, and the way they flit from interest to interest like a butterfly. Their usual flair for getting on with other people, and their typical charm and affability, ensure that they always have innumerable friends and always plenty to do and occupy themselves with. One problem that is likely to crop up will be the necessity for them to maintain a reasonable balance between their school and college commitments and their social lives, which may well be active, to say the least!

It is clear that the adolescent stage carries *choleric* overtones. Young people tend to be ardent and forceful, thrusting and ambitious, not to mention self-centred, whatever basic temperament they possess. It is the time for being rebellious, defiant and unruly, adventurous, courageous, audacious, dauntless and daring. Now is the time for working their way round the world for a year or two, doing voluntary work at home or overseas, and so on. Utopia is just around the corner, and their idealism is still strong and keen; the world is a rotten place and they are going to change things for the better. Challenges, difficulties and dangers there may be, but these are there to be met, and the inevitable obstacles and hindrances to be cleared away or brushed aside. Defiance is the keynote, so it's the time for joining every forward-looking society or organization there is, which they will support by protest marching, picketing, demonstrating, canvassing, fasting, working for nothing – anything to make the world a better place.

Middle age is characterized by traits that are *melancholic* in nature. Ambition, drive and aspirations fade and disappear, and a certain mood of resignation and bowing to the inevitable comes to the fore. With the bloom of youth a mere memory, the zeal for success and accomplishment, fortune-making and prosperity, affluence and opulence gradually diminishes. The obvious signs of advancing years and loss of physical attractiveness have to be accepted, and with this the usual disappointments associated with middle-age spread and its consolidation. That promotion never did come, and someone else snatched that opportunity before you could. You thought, with the children now grown up, that your problems would be over, or at least fewer. But oh, no, Sod's Law ensured that other difficulties crop up, and predicaments you never thought possible appeared out of the blue. Then there are the grandchildren... Introversion and a strong tendency towards nostalgia become more plainly discernible, and with memories of past experiences, and reflection on them, the dominant mood is one of submissiveness. Ah, well, thank goodness there's the pension...

As we get older still, it is the *phlegmatic* nature in all of us that takes over. We retire into ourselves – but make sure that we have plenty in the way of creature comforts. The days of strenuous sports and pastimes are over, and now that we haven't got to get up and go to work every day, we can take a lie-in whenever we feel like it. No more commuting, no more crowds and traffic to cope with, not to mention the weather... Yes, retirement is definitely preferable to all that! Should have retired earlier, of course. Much easier to plan the shopping now – can't say we miss the weekend hassles and having to get to the shops early to avoid the rush and the queues. There's more time to browse around the drinks shelves nowadays, and it would be rather nice to try a bottle or two of that Australian Chardonnay, or maybe a can or six of that Polish Pilsner. We haven't had time before now really to inspect what the delicatessen counter has on show. It's always nice to have something tempting in the fridge or freezer – you know, just for when we feel fanciful! Spoiling ourselves, did you say? Well, it's only money, after all, and you can't take it with you, can you?

And so comes the traditional time for passing on a few gems of life-wisdom to the younger folk. Well, offering them, anyway...

3. The Choleric Temperament

Motto   When the going gets tough, the tough get
             going.
Theme Tune   *My Way*

How to recognize a choleric person

As mentioned in Chapter 2 the choleric temperament
was associated in the mind of the Ancient Greeks with
the element of Fire, and considered to have taken on
many of its characteristics in terms of behaviour.
Excitable, impulsive, restless, often fiery-tempered and
aggressive, people with this temperament do indeed
remind us of leaping flames, hot and challenging as
they are, and it comes as no surprise that in tradition
it is linked with our blood and its characteristics. No-
one could ever accuse choleric people of having cold
natures; indeed, their behaviour could be summed up in
what is generally understood by the word 'hot-blooded'.
   Choleric people of both sexes are mostly short
and stocky in build, wide and square at the shoulders, thickset and with short necks, often giving the
impression of being stunted. They are invariably
well-muscled, hardy individuals, people with stamina
and strength. Their features are usually regular, with
well-formed foreheads and eyes that hold the other
person's in a sure and steady gaze, defiant or even
challenging, perhaps glinting with an inner light. The
nose is short, often with flared nostrils, but usually
well-formed. The lips are full and red, and the general complexion ruddy, but sometimes flushed. The

chin is well-formed and often prominent, and the line of the jaw strong and firm.

Male cholerics are often attractive to the opposite sex by reason of their sheer masculinity, and they often have the kind of rugged good looks regarded by many as handsome. They believe that the age of chivalry is by no means past, and are usually considerate and gallant in their attitude towards ladies of all ages. Choleric women are not dainty and fragile as a rule, and appear by no means helpless or delicate. On the contrary, they possess a certain air of solidity, reliability and dependability. This is not to say that they are incapable of graceful movements, as they often make good dancers. But it must not be forgotten that they can and do, in certain trying circumstances, act with unladylike aggressiveness, and are even capable of uttering choice Anglo-Saxon expletives. Indeed, both sexes are capable of this kind of behaviour, particularly when they are thwarted in their plans, or frustrated in carrying them out. At such times they are better left severely alone!

Cholerics are recognizable from a distance by their gait, which is firm and resolute, heel down first, each step being planted deliberately and firmly, even heavily, in a purposeful, often rapid stride. They give the impression of being in a hurry, which they often are, as they cannot wait to tackle the next job, overcome the next obstacle, win the next battle. Their body and limb movements are characteristically quick, sure and decisive, and their reflexes are excellent. They are typically persons of *action*, those whom you can rely on to get on with the job. Folk wisdom claims that if you want anything done, give it to a busy person – and that busy person will almost certainly turn out to be a choleric.

They are essentially unstable in their psychological make-up, and are, as you must have guessed by now, highly extroverted and unarguably divergent in their general approach to life. They tend to live life in the fast lane, and are prone to high blood pressure and its consequences. By nature energetic and hardworking, they are inclined to be harder on themselves than on others, and apply higher standards to themselves than to others, for they, quite as a matter of course, regard themselves as being superior. Boasting and bragging is not usually part of their make-up, however. They usually know their strengths and weaknesses, and are competent at what they do; otherwise, they would not be doing it. They are natural leaders, and they know it, taking charge without hesitation in emergencies and tight situations, when their resourcefulness and imaginative grasp of the circumstances come into their own.

Positive – and negative – characteristics

An outstanding attribute of people who have this temperament as predominant is their considerable strength of will. Their determination and go-ahead ways very often reveal themselves as stubbornness, obstinacy, pig-headedness or sheer cussedness – even bloody-mindedness. But they are usually cheerful, amiable and optimistic, ambitious and anxious to do well and succeed, and this means that they are invariably looking ahead to the future. They are always making plans, and if the wherewithal in terms of finance is forthcoming, the result is often a new enterprise in some shape or form, and frequently backing up these plans are fine qualities of courage, leadership, perseverance, self-sacrifice and devotion to duty.

There is no such word as 'can't' in the vocabulary of cholerics, and they relish anything in the nature of a challenge – so there's a tip for any woman who wants something done around the house! "Get out of the way and let me do it!" is the choleric's war-cry. There's no messing about where they're concerned, and it's far better to leave them to get on with it, which they invariably will – and you may count on them to make every effort to do a good job, quickly and cheerfully, if rather impatiently. And remember – they've got to have their own way. To start giving advice and unhelpful suggestions would be bad enough; but to criticise the work in progress would be taken as an invitation to them to throw down their tools and storm off, angrily rejecting your advice. This will probably be accompanied by pointed suggestions as to what you can do with it in a none too complimentary manner! So beware of quarrelsome cholerics!

Never forget that they fondly imagine that they are infallible, indispensable, invincible, considering no challenge too much for them. To tell them, even in joke, that they are 'past it', not up to the task, or even worse that they are failures, is like the shadow of doom itself to them. Their immediate reaction would be one of angry defiance, perhaps followed by bluster and bluff. If, however, they are forced to admit that they were wrong after all, and that their judgement was faulty; and if people try to belittle them scornfully and derisorily, their whole personality could collapse. And a once all-conquering choleric in a state of collapse is a sorry sight indeed, whichever way it occurs. Either they will get into an uncontrollable rage, perhaps becoming violently aggressive, when they are capable of ruthless brutality, or they will sink into a condition of most abject misery, full of self-pity, and caring for nothing and nobody, slinking away in dejection and despondency to lick the very real wounds that their pride and self-esteem have suffered.

So let them get on with the job. Offer to labour for them by all means – but keep your advice to yourself until it is asked for! And try to remember another golden rule when handling cholerics – if ever they would admit to being 'handled', except by members of the opposite sex – and that is to show appreciation for their efforts. Once you are in their good books, there is nothing they wouldn't do for you, no lengths to which they would not go to please you. But remember that cholerics like their – often not inconsiderable – worth to be recognized, and perhaps even to be admired. All this is good for their sizeable ego, and they thrive on it, usually without becoming arrogant, even if from their behaviour they may appear to be so.

But here a word of warning is necessary. However much they like their honest efforts to please to be appreciated, they cannot and will not tolerate flattery, 'creeping', 'flannelling' or other fawning, obsequious behaviour, so *never* try anything on in the nature of these. If you are guilty of anything like these, you will be met with contempt and rejection, and they will despise you. Most cholerics are 'honest John' types, people of integrity and honour, sincere and full of goodwill and the milk of human kindness. Although outwardly they often appear brusque and offhand, they are in reality goodhearted and kind, and can be very generous in all respects, and chivalrous as well. It is very rare for cholerics to kick people when they are down; if they do, rest assured that such treatment is well deserved.

This suggests that cholerics like to have their own way, and because they invariably possess very healthy, strong egos, this is how they think it should be by right! But don't forget that they are people of initiative and drive, the original 'self-starters', bold, fearless, and adventurous, often finding it difficult to see the difference between bravery and foolhardiness. Natural fighters, they are imaginative, inventive and resourceful, brooking no opposition. They will admit to being hasty some-times, and maybe just a little rash, but their intentions are honourable – as a rule! They are usually capable of balancing the risks before taking a chance, with every resolve to succeed. They certainly possess the unfailing optimism that is so often necessary for success.

Being natural leaders and born entrepreneurs, cholerics are commanding and self-assured, quick to grasp ideas, size up situations, and seize opportu-nities. Quick off the mark, energetic, forceful, imaginative, dependable and reliable, they see clearly the way ahead – and go for it! As I mentioned earlier, they do not suffer fools gladly, and considering them-selves as being more competent and efficient, cannot tolerate inefficiency and incompetence in others. They have a natural eye for detail, and have strong powers of concentration and application to the task. Often critical of others, they themselves do not take kindly to criticism. They like to be *boss*, and don't you forget it! Don't bother about explaining how you would do the job – it's got to be done their way – or else! So don't

ever try anything on without their sanctioning it first.
And don't expect them to 'go by the book', for they
are individualists through and through.

Relishing as they do challenge in any shape or form,
cholerics often find themselves in charge of businesses
and other enterprises, whether as managers, executives
or owners. When everything is going right, everything
is fine. They are then models of consideration and
concern for everyone. But when things go wrong – look
out! There is ranting and raving, shouting and thumping of desks. Everyone scatters, knowing the measure
of the wrath to come. The salespeople are lazy! The
financial managers thieves and rogues! Computer
operators? Careless and slack, of course. The factory
foremen and chargehands neglect their duties! The shop-
floor workers are idle layabouts. What does anyone care
about except their fat pay-packets! Everybody is to
blame but themselves – and so on, and so on.

If the company is found to be struggling to survive,
perhaps in hock to the banks and financiers, the kind of
'choleric collapse' described above is the likely consequence. The company is in ruins, and all because of his
incompetent staff. Of course it just had to happen when
he was cruising the Caribbean in his yacht together with
a few business cronies. It was impossible to leave the
place – what an idiot to think that he dare take a holiday!
As soon as his back was turned, etc ... but having little
memory of when, eighteen months before, he flew into
a rage and sacked his chief executive for doing nothing
more criminal than warning him that if things were
allowed to go on as they were going...

Choleric people possess a strong sense of individuality; they are, so to speak, undoubtedly 'their own
person', decisive, self-assured, self-confident – but also,

perhaps, self-willed, self-assertive, self-opinionated, masterful, domineering, and sometimes aggressive to the point of being pugnacious. A six-foot-six choleric rugby player in a bad temper is certainly a character to be avoided! Self-control is not such a fellow's strongest point, and it is this very quality, it would seem, that they have come down to Earth to learn!

Quite often cholerics have as the secondary temperament the melancholic, and this combination often serves to characterize the typical *manic-depressive* person. Cholerics are always exhibiting behaviour that is – well, ever so slightly, perhaps – that of a maniac! They are habitually accompanied by a sense of euphoria connected with past achievements and future conquests, and the unwavering single-mindedness that accompanies this, often to an excessive degree. When failure comes, as of course it is bound to from time to time, the depressive state descends, and with it whingeing self-pity and self-deprecation. The sorrows of Satan are minor affairs compared with those endured by choleric-melancholics in full descent into their self-induced, apparently bottomless pits of woe. But if you wait long enough, the old optimism will return, new ideas will form, fresh energies will stir, and before you know where you are, they are halfway through their next self-appointed task.

4. The Sanguine Temperament

Motto   Promises, promises!
Theme tune   *Blue Skies*

Sanguines are not easy to recognize

The sanguine temperament is associated with the element of Air, and with its flighty attributes not only reminiscent of both the wind currents in their way-wardness, but also the birds and butterflies which make use of them. Just as gravity is represented in the melancholics, so the opposite quality of *levity* is to be found in so many ways in sanguine people. Although the term 'sanguine' possesses strong conno-tations of blood, this is more because of the fact that it is in constant movement, and because of its facility to run 'hot' or 'cold'. These are useful concepts to remember with regard to this temperament, for they are all very apt. Many people with this as their main temperament are remarkably birdlike in their habitual gestures, quick and nervous in their movements, with every nerve constantly strained to its utmost.

As befits these general characteristics, their physical build is – at least until middle-age spread asserts itself – slender and harmoniously proportioned. Furthermore, they are often recognizable by their light, springy step alone, and their graceful movements. It should not be surprising, therefore, that most male as well as female fashion models are sanguines, appearing at their best on the catwalk! Generally of fair complexion, and blue-eyed, the gentlemen are

more often than not handsome, and the ladies beautiful, with heart-shaped or oval faces. Their features
are finely sculptured, their eyes expressive, lively and
sparkling under regular, well-arched eyebrows. The
nose is particularly significant: if it is snub or retroussé,
slightly turned up at the tip, perhaps aquiline, or even
larger than normal, and if there is other complementary
evidence, suspect a sanguine temperament.

Both melancholic and sanguine people are of the so-
called 'ectomorphic' (light or lean) type of physique,
and this can lead to some confusion between the two.
Normally, melancholics are taller, and have a slower,
heavier gait, and often with cast-down gaze, whereas
sanguines are much lighter and nimbler, inclined to
walk on their toes. Moreover, they are altogether more
lively, looking around them all the time and, birdlike,
constantly aware of what is going on around them.
Window-shopping is a favourite pastime of sanguine
people, who are ever on the lookout for the new, the
curious and the quaint, for they take an interest in
everything – but only for a short time!

Needless to say, they are extremely fashion-con-
scious, possess flair and panache, and keep well up
to date in that respect. Impressionable themselves, they
love to make an impression on others, whether appropriate or not, and the ladies find the temptation to
acquire jewellery and accessories by the drawerful very
hard to resist. However, sanguine people of both
sexes invariably possess good taste, being artistic by
nature and divergent in their basic attitudes. Add to all
this every social grace in the book, and considerable
charm into the bargain, and it is easy to see why they
easily outstrip the other temperaments in sheer sociability. They make excellent companions, being typically

amiable, congenial and good-natured, and their natural conviviality ensures that they are never short of friends and acquaintances. They can generally be relied upon to be the 'life and soul' of every party.

All this sounds as if sanguine people are God's gift to the human race, but of course there are certain drawbacks to this seeming perfection! Impressionable and nervous, imaginative and inventive, they are also notoriously unreliable, as their mood changes as rapidly as the wind. Expect an inability to be punctual as a matter of course; and impatient and lacking in endurance themselves, they expect other people to be models of dependability and endurance. This certain lack of 'stickability' amounts to a serious temperamental flaw. They are greatly hampered by their sheer lack of concentration, of the ability to focus their attention unwaveringly on anything. Thoughts, ideas and impressions replace one another with extreme rapidity in the mind of sanguine people, and as their memory is not exceptionally retentive, they often find it very difficult to absorb subject-material of any substance. Studying , being essentially repetitive and long-term, and demanding of considerable powers of self-discipline, they find tiresome and irritating. The ability to tolerate constant repetition by way of revision and practice of any body of knowledge, or practical skill that has to be thoroughly learned, may well remain undeveloped for this very reason.

Sanguines make poor scholars because of their weak memories and superficial approach, for they scarcely ever find the capacity for studying anything in depth. Instead of logical procedures of thinking and deduction, they rely on their not inconsiderable powers of intuition. They seem to have an instinctive ability for penetrating to the heart of a problem, and their exceptional powers of discrimination and evaluation come to their aid in weighing up its pros and cons. Perceptive and quick-witted, they have a sharp eye for anything that is incongruous, and they make excellent critics for this reason. Experience is doubtless the best teacher where sanguines are concerned, for they thereby learn things which they didn't deliberately set out to! Pain and woe are their frequent companions, and for this reason they need all their ample reserves of adaptability and resilience, not to mention optimism and the gift of forgetfulness. With increasing years, they accumulate considerable life-wisdom which they have generally acquired the hard way, and so make first-class grandparents!

Changeable, and themselves loving change, sanguines invariably find it difficult to stick to a task *and get it finished*. Their stereotype is the well-known one of the Jack-of-all-trades who is master of none. When something novel comes their way, their enthusiasm and zeal know no bounds; and you may be sure that they look upon the latest gadget or knick-knack they have acquired as the best thing since sliced bread! In the homes of most sanguines furniture is periodically changed around, ornaments and pictures re-arranged on the walls, and new curtains fitted. Articles which they have grown bored with are thrown out, and new ones appear. If money is short or not, sanguines genuinely enjoy going through the rails of their local charity shops for the real bargains they find there. A welcome bonus to this is a warm inner glow, for they are not exactly strangers to the questionable delights associated with extravagance. Money management is not their strongest talent by any means!

"Just look at that!"

Sanguine people have a fascination for everything new or unusual, and whatever this may be, it is of course very much the flavour of the month – for its enchantments will not usually last much longer than that! Their interest as well as knowledge is more often than not merely superficial, and they acquire much by means of hearsay and gossip. Being excellent conversationalists, often brilliant and witty, and good story tellers, they are apt to pass off what smatterings of information they have acquired as part of their own repertoire, for all sanguines are accomplished actors. Gifted with captivating ways, they find it easy to exploit the gullible, bedazzling the rest of us with their usual magnetism and charm. Diamonds are indeed a sanguine girl's best friend, for their ever-changing glitter will be one of the few things that will *never* pall!

They are frequently interested in everything, but their interest does not persist; they all too soon find another interest, then another, and yet another, in an exhausting series of efforts which remain essentially fruitless in terms of results. They do not usually take very kindly to anything in the way of manual labour, and they all too often produce 'rush jobs' which are anything but satisfactory. Near enough is indeed good enough – for them! Preparation is hurried and/or non-existent, and after the job has been done – if it ever gets done, that is – someone else is left to tidy up. If lights are left burning in an empty room, if doors remain unshut, if there are muddles everywhere, if meals are undercooked or overcooked, letters unanswered and bills unpaid, you may be reasonably sure that the culprit is sanguine in temperament.

As you may have gathered already, sanguine people are not exceptionally strong-willed or determined. Many of their actions betray an inconsistency which puzzles others of less changeable temperament, and they make fine mimics and impressionists. Many sanguines are vacillating and indecisive in their ways, and their feelings are also constantly variable. You may be talking to a sanguine person, sharing with them something which you find interesting, and which you think will interest them too, only to find almost immediately that they haven't taken in a word you've said, in spite of their nods and smiles of acknowledgement. Indeed, they may turn away, even before you have finished a sentence, to interrupt a conversation with someone else on the other side of the room! Their ways of thinking and doing are sometimes strangely self-contradictory, to the point of deceiving others as well as themselves.

Also, they possess the curious propensity, once they have a plan for a project, immediately to imagine that it is already done! It is – *in their minds* – but very often such plans are never realised. Everything, so to speak, must be done yesterday! They are very much inclined to take life as it comes, and therefore do not bother too much with making elaborate plans for the future, much less with carrying them out. Luckily for them, they possess the necessary optimism and flexibility to cope with all the changes they bring about. They know very well that they are capable of attempting to change horses in mid-stream, and how useless it is to try and fix *anything* in concrete.

A notable characteristic of most sanguine people is that of being to a considerable extent affected by their social milieu, by the company that they keep. They often take on the qualities and attributes of those around them, whether of partner, friends or family. This is doubtless partly due to their impressionable nature, but also because they are so changeable and imitative. They seem to have a need for someone in the nature of a hero or heroine to look up to and admire, and perhaps model themselves on. This kind of adulation may well extend to sporting, showbiz and other celebrities, but all too often they find that such figures have feet of clay – yet another event to write off to experience.

These kinds of attitude are perfectly in accord with those young in heart, and also of all young people, whose basic temperament is always overlaid by sanguine properties during their impressionable years. (cf. Chapter 2) Other characteristics also point to the wish of all sanguines to preserve their youth for all time, with the consequence that if you see a ewe dressed up as lamb, she is bound to be a sanguine! And as for overgrown youths with pony-tails, middle-aged men wearing tight jeans, and ancient schoolboys in shorts sportingly exhibiting their varicose veins to all and sundry – well!

Being highly sociable, by this very definition they have a natural love and concern for the human race at large, and as a rule their social consciences are keen. Sanguine people are sensitive and kind, sincere in their good wishes for the welfare of everyone, particularly "the stranger within our gates". It is they whose coins find their way into the busker's hat, and who cannot bear to pass by the Salvation Army, Red Cross, or any other charity collector who gives them a smile. Their depth of feeling may not be more than that of sentiment, but they are sympathetic as well as empathic, and their heart is invariably in the right place.

Possessors of other temperaments would do well to remember always to treat sanguines kindly, for then they will respond to you in like manner. Capricious they may be, and irritating with it, but never forget that whatever mood they are in, and however disagreeable at the time, that it will pass. Be firm by all means, for by doing so you may well be providing the very anchor they need at that particular time, but do try to keep your annoyance, and above all your temper, to yourself. If you lose your self-control, they will not like you, and moreover will not respect you for it – and don't forget that they want to hold you in esteem. Whatever else, do not try to throw your weight about, browbeat, threaten or attempt to domineer sanguine people. If you do, they will laugh at you and ridicule you, for they are free spirits who will not be bound. So don't try anything on in the shape of emotional or other blackmail, much less physical violence; for if you do, you may lose them for ever.

Remember always that our typical sanguine is sensitive and easily hurt, and their heart is easily touched. Rather, bring them little gifts, surprise them now and again with acts of thoughtfulness and concern – and never forget their birthday!

They rarely bear any trivial grudge for long, for their innate good nature usually takes over. However, if the insult or injury is a serious one, then you will never find anyone more vengeful, vindictive and unforgiving that a sanguine person who feels that they have been wronged. But even they get over this eventually, let bygones be bygones and as always put it down to experience, as another addition to their ever-growing store of life-wisdom.

5. The Phlegmatic Temperament

Motto   Procrastinate tomorrow!
Theme Tune   *Home, Sweet Home*

Identifying the typical phlegmatic

The archetypal symbol of this temperament is Water, and it is a worthwhile one to reflect on. As mentioned earlier, water always seeks its own level, and practically every characteristic of phlegmatic people reflects this flatness – except their physical shape! A calm sea is remarkable for its seeming lack of movement, at least on the surface; but we know that there are always undercurrents to beware of! This formlessness, this evenness of appearance and character are typical of both. Mentally and emotionally, phlegmatic people appear to be for the most part flat and uninteresting, featureless and unexciting. But they, like the oceans themselves, have hidden depths which conceal a whole world which is hidden to others, and remains so – except to the favoured few to whom they allow the privilege of exploring them.

Most people think of their body as being solid, but it is well known that we are composed mostly of water – or at least fluids of some sort or other. It is in these body fluids that phlegmatics feel, as it were, most at home – particularly in their digestive juices! It is not by chance that these 'fat and jolly' stereotypes are built as they are – more for comfort than speed! At mealtimes they are instantly recognizable by their reverential attitude to the comestibles set before them, complemented by the

customary flavoursome fluids. When a plate laden with
food is placed before a phlegmatic individual, their
eyes devour the food before even a fork is lifted. Any
conversation – which in any case will be frugal – comes
to an end until well after the food has disappeared. They
are natural gourmets – or, if their taste is more for
quantity than quality, natural gourmands. Whatever
their level of appreciation, to phlegmatics partaking of
food and drink is almost a sacred rite, to be accorded the
highest respect and adulation. The wise among women
know this, for in very deed the way to a man's heart is
through his stomach!

Phlegmatics are similar in general bodily appearance to the cholerics, that is to say, inclined to be short
and stocky. Such similarities may not be so apparent at
a distance, but when they get closer, the differences
become very clear. Whereas the cholerics are 'square',
the phlegmatics are 'round'; the former hard and well-
muscled, the latter inclined to be round-shouldered,
soft and flabby. The cholerics move quickly and
purposefully, whereas the phlegmatics move around
ponderously and slowly by comparison, and this is
reflected in their gait. They give the impression of being
clumsy, and they often have a shambling, slouching
way of walking, as if they cannot adapt themselves to
the ground under their feet.

Often plump or even portly, especially after the
dreaded 'middle-age spread' stage has been reached,
they present an air of unruffled, imperturbable calm,
which they wish to preserve. They will go to
considerable lengths in order to safeguard this
particular evenness of atmosphere, as they love quiet
and tranquillity, for they never get tired of their own
company. Because of this they run the risk of appearing

stupid and witless, dull and unresponsive, and many phlegmatics go in danger of being labelled 'thick' because of their reluctance to be drawn into tittle-tattle, gossip or trivial talk. They have an intense and strong inner life, and possess an over-riding desire to maintain their inner harmony and peace, which they long to extend to the outer world, which as we all know, will have none of it! Their patience and forbearance are considerable, and their tolerance levels are extraordinarily high, far higher than those of any of the other temperaments.

In repose, which they most often are, their roundish facial features are generally indeterminate, immobile and impassive. Their eyes are often dull and rather watery, with a disinterested gaze almost entirely lacking in expression. The nose is invariably short, sometimes bulbous, or at least fleshy, and per-haps wide at the nostrils, and not to be mistaken for the more well-defined nose of cholerics. The lips are usually full, but tend to be lacking in the firmness of line which is also characteristic of choleric people. The often strident tones of the latter contrast with the lower pitch and tone of the phlegmatics, whose speech is inclined to be slow, perhaps hesitant or halting. The chin is often rounded, lacking in firmness; and in later life it is common for that chin to become a double one, for obvious reasons!

"I just can't be bothered"

That statement sums up most phlegmatic people's general attitude to the majority of situations, except of course mealtimes! They are often untidily or even shabbily dressed, habitually putting on what they

wore yesterday, and the day before that. They grow
fond of that easy-fitting jacket or those cosy, well-worn
slippers, and stick with them. What does it matter to
anyone else as long as they are comfortable, and as
for fashion – well, that's for fools! Contrary to
following fashion, they are reluctant to draw attention
to themselves by dressing in any way but modestly
and conventionally. Why change for the sake of it?
If they had their way, nothing – but nothing – would
ever change! They do not like change, and although
perhaps not bothering to go so far as to hate it, this
is the impression they give. They are therefore inclined
to be old-fashioned and stuck in their ways, reluctant
to try anything new or unfamiliar. The furniture, pictures and ornaments must be replaced exactly where
they were before redecoration, for instance, which of
course would have to resemble previous colour schemes,
patterns and so on.

If you accuse phlegmatics to their face that they are
dull, uninteresting people, they will not be at all an-
noyed or put out. Their reaction will be a gentle smile,
perhaps, and a dreamy look will show in their eyes
which bespeaks a wonderful, secret world which their
accuser knows not of, but would like to know. Try
asking a phlegmatic what their day has been like, and
the answer will invariably be: "Oh, alright." When
pressed for details about what actually happened, the
answer will again be non-committal: "Oh, nothing
much." No crumbs of information will be forthcoming
from them unless they are pestered for them. If you try
deliberately to provoke them you will have to try very
hard indeed; and if you make hurtful remarks – to which
they are *very* sensitive – they will turn away from you in
sorrow and pity. If you wrong them, they will 'clam up',

refusing to discuss matters, or even to speak at all. Often accused of sulking as a consequence of this kind of thing, they will deny this. They merely want to think things over quietly and thoroughly, and ask for the peace in which to do so. They merely wish to be left alone, which is surely not too much to ask for...

To feel *secure* is the overwhelming desire and need of phlegmatics, and this is why they wish to preserve the status quo, for the unknown or unfamiliar tends to disturb their equilibrium and they feel most discomfited when this occurs. In fact, they do not like any kind of disturbance, from a ringing telephone to an unexpected visitor; to them this kind of thing is an intrusion on their privacy – and there can be no more private person than a phlegmatic. You may count yourself as honoured and privileged if you are one of those rare people to whom they will open up and discuss their thoughts and feelings – for they do have feelings! If information or an opinion is insisted upon, or worse still demanded, phlegmatics are thrown into confusion, and the results are generally far from satisfactory. They like to have due notice, so that they can mentally prepare themselves, for such preparation for whatever situation is a necessity for them if things are to go right and best.

Never guilty of being balls of fire or bundles of energy, phlegmatics give the impression of being passive to the extent of laziness, which is indeed their usual fault. This all too often deteriorates into idleness and sheer inactivity, and the world's champion couch potato has got to be a phlegmatic! Very close to resembling the 'Andy Capp' stereotype, a severe case of phlegmaticitis would find its 'sufferer' sprawled in their favourite armchair, with a table on the left covered with empty crisp/biscuit/chocolate/sweet wrappings (more underneath it, of course!), and the table on the right hidden under empty glasses, cups, bottles, tins, etc., also with reserve supplies to hand beneath it. Their usual ample proportions do not arise from their taking too much in the way of exercise – except perhaps that of the right arm!

They seldom take the initiative in anything except where food and drink is concerned, mainly because they have such little confidence in their own abilities. Always modest to the point of self-effacement, their main problem lies in their liability to develop an inferiority complex. Consequently, they are rarely to be found in positions of leadership or responsibility unless their secondary temperament happens to be choleric, when the best of all possible worlds obtains. Followers rather than leaders therefore, they are good at taking orders; moreover, they can be depended upon to carry them out to the letter. Introduced to a new job or new procedures, they may be slow to absorb fresh information, because they require time to think, prepare themselves, and perhaps need to have a dummy run or two before settling in. Like the proverbial elephant, they may be slow to learn, per-haps, but they never forget. They know that practice makes perfect, and if the task is within their capabilities, perfection will eventually come, for they take due pride in a job well done. They are careful, conscientious, meticulous workers and craftspeople who, with their characteristically strong sense of duty, do their very best to please at all times.

Somewhat lacking in imagination, they are thor-oughly honest and trustworthy for the most part, and utterly reliable and dependable. Lacking as they do imagination and creativity, it would not occur to them to enter into anything like embezzlement or connivance of any kind, for they go by the book, obey the law and follow the rules. Give them reasonably comfortable working conditions, with regular tea-breaks and a full lunch-hour, and you will have methodical, painstaking employees, who in their serene contentment can be relied on to co-operate in everything short of the downright criminal. They invariably make good, loyal and faithful employees.

As might be expected, phlegmatic people are best suited for work that is routine or repetitive, in which care and exactness are of paramount importance, and preferably where they can work at their own pace. They can usually be relied on not to get into a 'flap', get excited or panicky if there is an emergency of some kind, for they are perfectly capable of rising to the occasion when that occasion demands a cool response. This is not to say that they enjoy such experiences, of course; they merely do what has to be done, with their customary efficiency and attention to detail. They are best suited to being 'back-room boys', away from involvement with the public, and left to work on their own, which they may perfectly well be trusted to do. Among all the temperaments, the phlegmatic is the most predictable in terms of behaviour and responses.

You may think that, unsociable and inwardly turned as they are, phlegmatic people are boring, dull, miserable killjoys, with never a smile within a mile; but in this you would be very much in error. Do not underestimate their capabilities. They can match the charm of any sanguine or choleric if they choose to be disarming. With a well-enjoyed meal tucked away, not to mention a convivial glass or two of your choicest wine or best malt whisky, they will often be found to be witty and amusing, and good listeners always. Always kindly disposed, helpful and considerate, they have a genuinely sympathetic ear for all those in trouble, and generally have good advice to give – if asked for, that is. They spend much of their time pondering and reflecting, contemplating and meditating on things, turning them over and over in their minds; but the results of these cogitations are often never uttered to anyone, for their innate modesty and shyness forbids this. They rarely break into conversation or discussion, and if they do bother to attend meetings of any kind will speak only if no-one else has put the same point of view as their own, and then only if they feel exceptionally strongly about whatever matter is under review.

One of their least desirable characteristics is their indecisiveness; for when faced with a number of options, they often have the greatest difficulty in making up their minds. For this reason they may well ask a partner or friend to help them do so, or even make up their minds for them. This can be extremely trying because advice given to them can confuse them further, and is usually rejected anyway! Conventional in their tastes, and reserved in their thinking, they will certainly avoid anything that smacks of the novel or original. People who know them well realize this, of course, so that there is never much question of persuasion. Fast-talking salespeople are wasting their time on phlegmatics, for they immediately grow suspicious of such people's motives. Their natural caution asserts itself, and they imagine that there might just be an ulterior motive behind all that smooth talk. Perhaps that secondhand car that is being 'pushed' at them has hidden rust, or a worn engine; that seeming bargain on the street stall may have, as they say, fallen off the back of a lorry; and that, to straight-laced phlegmatics, would never do!

Thrifty by instinct, they have keen judgement where money is concerned, and know its value. With typical caution they methodically check their bills, reconcile their bank statement every month, save for that rainy day, and salt away all that they can possibly spare. Purchases are invariably made only after much forethought and relative comparisons, and people of this temperament will not in any circumstances allow themselves to be rushed into buying anything. Most phlegmatics are good at doing their homework, and knowing full well that there is no substitute for quality, they invariably go for it. They believe in the tried and trusted, that which has proved its worth by standing the test of time. What if it is old-fashioned? Don't people know what *antiques* are? So the cheap and flashy, the trendy and ostentatious, is not for them, you may be sure.

To coin a phrase: if you persuade phlegmatics against their will, they'll be of the same opinion still. Their toleration level is pretty high, but they cannot stand being pestered or badgered into making any decision or changing their mind, not to mention attempts at coercion or bullying in any shape or form. If people persist with this kind of thing, then they may succeed in making them angry, and when thoroughly roused or provoked they are capable of extremely violent behaviour. It is a matter of the worm eventually turning. Long-suffering and patient they may well be, but parallel with this goes a certain stubbornness and intractability which can be a source of much irritation to family and friends. So often fixed in their attitudes, they are frequently impervious to advice and comment – favourable or unfavourable – not to mention criticism, however constructive.

However, being reasonable for the most part, they will recognize their own limitations in these respects, and will give in if they think they can benefit by it in some way.

As mentioned earlier, laziness is always a constant danger, and this usually stems from disinterest and apathy, which are other undesirable attributes. The simple truth is, all too often, that phlegmatics, as ever, simply cannot be bothered. They complain so little – what's the use of complaining? – that they may well allow others to walk all over them, and unashamedly take advantage of them. To many people the typical phlegmatic person, although easy to recognize after comparatively little observation, is an enigma. He or she may appear simple and uncomplicated at first sight, but rest assured that behind those mild eyes and placid features is a very complex character indeed.

6. The Melancholic Temperament

Motto   Life is real, life is earnest.
Theme Tune   *Yesterday*

Recognizing a melancholic is no problem

The archetypal symbol in the case of people with the melancholic as their chief temperament is the heaviest of all the elements of Greek science, namely Earth. The most solid parts of our body are our teeth and bones; they are mineral, heavy, subject to the forces of gravity. Even the physical appearance of melancholics makes all this plain, for they go around as if they are carrying the weight of the world on their shoulders. They are usually tall and thin or wiry, gangling and loose-limbed, with characteristically long faces, and their movements are slow and heavy, deliberate and careful. With downcast gaze, sad-eyed and serious, the stooping shoulders and plodding gait make typical melancholics easy to spot, even from a distance.

They usually have smallish heads, somewhat narrow at the temples, and the facial features are invariably long and fine, most likely ending in a sharp, narrow chin. Their hair is frequently dark, wispy, sparse, and lank. The eyes, too, are usually dark, and carry a concerned, anxious, worried look, and the lines of the face are downdrawn, as is the whole facial expression. The nose is almost always long and thin, and the nostrils correspondingly narrow. A melancholic person's lips are generally thin and pale, in sharp contrast to, say, the full red lips of a typical choleric person. Their speech is usually slow, measured and low-pitched. Another clue to watch for is their tendency to hold their head to one side, giving the impression that it is too heavy to hold upright.

Being introverted like the phlegmatics, who are preoccupied with their sense of bodily well-being, melancholics are more engrossed in matters of the mind. Phlegmatics are stable in their characteristics, as we have seen, but by contrast melancholics are unstable, and it is not surprising that they live so intensely in their inner world, and are subject to moods, 'states' and emotional swings. Quiet and reserved in manner and reserved in demeanour, they tend to withdraw from the world, spending long hours pondering over real – or imagined – problems.

They very often hold the strange conviction that they have many more worries and anxieties than other people, and make no secret of this to those who are patient enough to listen. The truth is, of course, that their fears and trepidations are no greater in number or complexity than those of anyone who possesses nothing of the melancholic temperament in their make-up; merely that their sensitivities in these areas are keener. Such incidents or situations that would cause them apprehension and consternation would be dismissed as minor matters by non-melancholics, and taken in their stride.

Melancholics may even go out of their way to find things to worry about, for a certain perverseness emerges from time to time, and they make martyrs of themselves, wallowing in their pain and woe – and enjoying the sensation! Like the cholerics, they have an exceptionally strong sense of self – their ego, too, being inclined to be somewhat oversized. Whereas the cholerics go out to conquer the outer world, melancholics wrestle with problems arising in their inner world. Just as cholerics tend to domineer and lay down the law in their outer behaviour, shouting and thumping tables, melancholics get their own way by tyrannizing over their partners and friends in much subtler ways. The chief way of going about this is by *demanding attention*, for their main delusion – merely one of many, be it said – is that they are unquestionably the centre of the universe, and moreover deserve to be so. This kind of attitude reflects their likely susceptibility for developing an inferiority complex, because everyone else knows that they are not, so naturally they feel the urge to compensate for this.

Their more frequent complaint – and again only one of many – is that they are *misunderstood*. Nobody understands them, or is even capable of understanding them; they are too complex, too 'interesting', too 'special', and their individual genius simply too elevated for other mortals to comprehend. Just as cholerics tend to be outwardly arrogant, so the melancholics express their egotism in their manipulative behaviour. They quickly take hurt if people have the effrontery to pass them by, or worse still ignore them (too dull for typical sanguines) or treated with indifference (by apathetic phlegmatics). They are best handled by other melancholics, and you may be sure that a good time is then had by all. The latest 'disasters' have to be gone over in delicious detail, and their latest visits to their GPs minutely described, and any operations lovingly dwelt on, every drop of pathos and self-pity being lovingly squeezed out of every anguished minute in an orgy of mutual commiseration.

It is of course absolutely useless endeavour to try to cheer melancholics up when they are delighting in their latest attack of depression, or attempt to jolly them along, or encourage them to 'snap out of it'. They will have none of this because they do not wish it; they merely want to emphasise just how very special they are to be singled out for suffering in ways you and other mere mortals know not of. Practiced and experienced melancholics bewail their fate long and – well, not exactly – loud, for that, they know, would be ineffectual and even counter-productive. Their low, husky monotonous tones, breaking with feigned emotion now and again, will hold you as if hypnotized, for you cannot bear – nor would you dare – either to break in or break away!

No, the way ahead for you in such circumstances is to relate such a catalogue of real (or fictitious) woes with every ounce of pathos you can possibly muster. Putting your own temperament and other considerations aside, go into all the gory details of your own (or someone else's) sicknesses and sorrows, laying on the agony as thickly as you can. Reach for the box of tissues or flutter your handkerchief if you cannot feign tears! You will, almost invariably, be met with tender sympathy, heart-felt concern, genuine fellow-feeling. You will be offered help and advice; be given addresses of organizations to contact, individuals to write to, titles of magazines and books to consult – all with the sincerest of motives and the very best and kindest of intentions. Your heart will melt, of course, and any hard feelings you may have harboured for whingeing, self-pitying melancholics who are forever moaning and complaining, will fade.

It is invariably a good idea, if considered appropriate of course, to ask favours of melancholic people, and make demands on them; because if they consider your suffering to be greater than theirs, they will gallantly respond. The caring professions, particularly those in the realms of medicine and nursing, teaching, social and pastoral work are all satisfying for melancholics, and the world is better for their presence. Such kinds of vocation help them to overcome their intense egotism, their innate selfishness, for this is what they instinctively strive towards. By involving ourselves in the pain and suffering of others, we are all thereby ennobled, and this is why so many old people, and particularly those of melancholic disposition, have developed into fine and noble individuals, bearing that unmistakable air of serene goodwill to everyone, and have gained the power to bless.

All four temperaments present certain characteristic complications in terms of human relationships; individuals of whatever category could be designated as 'difficult to live with' for various reasons. Many people experience the seemingly everlasting mood of pessimism that overhangs melancholics much of the time as wearisome and wearing. The gloominess, the apprehensiveness and despair, the endless grousing and grumbling, and the demands for sympathy and pity, are more than most people can stand. Melancholics seem doomed to see only the dark sides of life, and just as it is useless to try and cheer them up, so it is to try to argue with them, appealing to reason in order to make them see and recognize their one-sided approach to life. This is just as impossible as trying to reason with a choleric person when they are in a towering rage!

Never forget that innate self-centredness, and make allowances for it. Melancholics fondly imagine that only they are privileged to know the *real* truth of things, and this is what makes them so self-opinionated, and desirous of being the focus of everyone else's attention as well as their own. As a result, their judgement can never be wrong. They are in their own eyes whiter than white, though sparing a passing gesture of pity for the rest of us who are of shades varying from grey to black. Obstinate to the point of pigheadedness, and firmly rooted in the typically introverted attitudes of self-centredness and self-interest, they are usually impervious to any argument – at least to begin with. If you persist in trying to reason, or argue your viewpoint, you will probably be ignored by some, but the more perceptive will listen to attempts at persuasion, as it demonstrates that you have taken an interest in them, and that pleases them, and flatters their ego.

"Nobody understands me!"

Melancholics have a way of seeking one another out, and if you don't belong to 'the club', that's just too bad for you – or so they think! Theirs is an endless, tireless search for sympathy or even pity, and above all *understanding*. Of course we all strive for this, but they seek it unrelentingly. They are usually quick to detect whether you are being insincere or superficial, and this does not please them. They love to feel safe and secure, and you may be sure that, like their fellow-introverts the phlegmatics, they approach every situation with extreme caution, keep a sharp eye on their finances, and are prepared for the inevitable rainy day, which is certain to arrive, if not tomorrow, then undoubtedly the day after!

With their innate yearning for and desire to achieve security, melancholic people do not like to be confronted with ideas or notions that may upset their status quo. Invariably, their religious beliefs, political leanings, and opinions on a thousand and one other matters will be fixed and rigid. They have got them, and they are going to keep them, regardless. So be careful, if you feel tempted to argue with them, not to point out the error of their ways in whatever direction, for they will not appreciate your solicitude, however kindly and sincerely meant. Always bear in mind that they are fundamentally *negative* in their characteristic attitudes, and are inclined to deny rather than affirm, particularly where their set views, beliefs or opinions are concerned. This stems largely from their almost obsessive desire for security at practically any cost, and in this they are very much like their introverted cousins, the phlegmatics.

Remember, too, that they like to have their own way, however seemingly meek and mild and long-suffering and patient they may appear. Far from the bullying, overbearing, blustering demands of the typical choleric, melancholics resort to more subtle, less spectacular subterfuges. If a melancholic woman does not wish to go out – or whatever! – she will most likely not resort to the hackneyed, cliché-like excuse of 'having a headache', appealing to the sympathy and finer feelings of her partner in more subtle or sophisticated ways. If she claims to feel somewhat indisposed – and melancholics are the world's most skilled and accomplished hypo-chondriacs – the complaint and its symptoms would of course have been well researched and rehearsed. This fact should certainly not prevent him from going out and enjoying *him*self. Of course she would simply *love* to go wherever or do whatever, and is sure that she would have enjoyed it, but she does not wish to spoil his fun – and so on.

This kind of deception does not seem to disturb their otherwise seemingly tender conscience, because it is perfectly possible for melancholics to worry and fret and actually *think* themselves into the conviction that they actually are unwell. They readily admit that they would not want to be the proverbial 'wet blanket' – not realizing that this is what they usually are anyway! Of course, she would enjoy her partner's attention and concern, going all helpless and wilting, thereby boosting his own sense of 'duty well and truly done', his own powers to comfort and console, and his own undoubted virtue of self-sacrifice. After all, his partner is manifesting this same meritorious behaviour by suffering at home, while he goes out to enjoy himself – and so the mutual admiration society is guaranteed steady progress!

This strange tendency to submit not only themselves but others to their own torment, is evidence of their basically ascetic natures. Sorrow and suffering are of course good for everyone, and we all know that there is no gain without pain. This being so, melancholics often seek situations in which genuine self-sacrifice is possible for them, or even certain.

Being familiar with real or imagined anguish and affliction, anxiety, distress and misery, they understand how sufferers feel, and will seek to alleviate such conditions. They are, quite literally, *born* philanthropists, voluntary aid workers, first aiders, charity supporters, fund-raisers for good causes and suchlike. They enjoy putting themselves out for others, and will go to endless trouble to give help and support to those in need.

The capacity for expressing mercy and compassion in practical terms is built into melancholic people, and if once they can subdue their own innately egotistic qualities, they are capable of developing the qualities of *un*selfishness to an extraordinary extent, and become worthy and meritorious agents of peace and goodwill in the world.

7. In the Workplace

What is good for the beehive is good for the bee

It goes without saying that in your place of work, whether office, factory or field, interpersonal relationships should be as harmonious as possible. Naturally, we all like to be happy in our work, and this being so, we are then always at our most productive. Inept and insensitive behaviour, just as much as poor strategies of communication, may hinder and even damage the efforts of those trying to maintain optimal contentment all round amongst colleagues. The word 'subordinate' should carry little or no force in the workplace, for in the last resort we are *all* dependent on one another, and there is really no room for posturing, the cultivating or pursuit of 'one-upmanship', excessive dependence on rank or status, and suchlike.

This mutual interdependence, and the social interaction that ensures its steady functioning, is more evident in some industrial or commercial organizations than others. It bears repetition that it always pays to keep people sweet, and not to get on the wrong side of them; and this is where a detailed knowledge of the characteristics of your colleagues' temperaments as well as your own can do much to keep friction at its minimum and smoothness of operations at its maximum. As I have already mentioned, it is your ability to predict typical reactions of an individual to given situations that is the measure of your understanding of the four temperaments.

Of course, whoever is chosen to do what must depend to a great extent on that person's aptitude, whether manual or intellectual – or both. A really thick and overbearing choleric, who 'bounces' the local Master of Foxhounds who is inadvertently late in arriving for the county hunt ball, can be as much a handicap in his fashion as a wizard of a melancholic accountant who, deranged on account of his melancholically induced anxiety and obsession concerning his own private finances, resorts to embezzlement. The temperaments that individuals possess determine their pre-dispositions for this kind of occupation or that, according to their basic traits, attributes and personal qualities. It is *how* they apply these that is really important, and as with 'horses for courses', there are distinct advantages when everything comes together in terms of temperament, skills and occupation, both for employer and employee.

The leopard and its spots

It bears repetition, too, that it is worse than useless, and a source of needless irritation and frustration, not to mention in every way counter-productive, to attempt to *change* an individual's temperament by any means. A leopard cannot and does not change its spots, so do not expect to achieve this. This is not to say that we cannot and do not modify our own characteristic behaviour, but in terms of the psychology of the temperaments, we *mature* as we grow in years and experience, and even life-wisdom. Our basic behavioural traits retain their essential attributes, even if we are able to modify them, refining them and realizing with increasing clarity and greater certainty how we can actually make use of them, and this applies to our secondary temperament too.

Over the years we learn how to integrate, in a perfectly natural way, our two main temperaments, calling upon which one we *need* in the handling of whatever particular situations or circumstances obtain at the time. If we can behave in a choleric fashion when we need to, for example in the event of an outbreak of fire or other emergency, that is to the benefit of all concerned. On the other hand, we may need to call upon our secondary phlegmatic temperament if we are faced with an over-persuasive salesman or an irate shop steward or foreman who appears at our door in a towering rage. *Then* is certainly not the time to be choleric! Remember that if sufficient self-discipline and self-control is forthcoming, we shall find that we can make good use of the qualities our secondary temperament can provide. Moreover, we shall be able to summon such attributes up almost at will, and on demand.

With experience and imagination, and the insights obtained from continual practice and perseverance, we shall eventually be able to call to our aid whatever qualities we need at the time which are to be found in our remaining two temperaments also. This kind of facility is admittedly difficult to achieve, but it will come with sufficient practice and perseverance, and the result will be a better balanced personality, less inner and outer discord, and greater benefits in terms of productivity and job satisfaction for everyone, leader and led alike.

Thus, if you are a choleric employer suddenly faced with a personnel 'incident' such as I have described, your ploy should always be to call upon your reserves of patience if your secondary temperament is phlegmatic, sympathy and fellow-feeling if it is melancholic, or exercise your conviction that no situation endures for ever if it is sanguine. A younger choleric person would possibly attack the situation with characteristic vigour, laying down the law in a display of histrionics, and set about sorting things out decisively and energetically. The result may be a temporarily restored harmony in the case of the work-force, but with an increase in their own blood-pressure! An older choleric person, whose temperament has matured, would undoubtedly take charge of the situation, but would, in addition to their ability to grasp the issues involved and see a possible solution, bring to bear on it their innate geniality, goodwill and resourcefulness. Such a person, by reason of their more balanced and serene attitudes, could hope to live to a ripe old age and not, by reason of heart attack or apoplexy, be compelled to make a premature departure from the Earth!

This kind of event gives the lie to the current fashion of regarding people over forty to be already 'past it'. On the contrary, those who are on the right side of forty know what their juniors do not, namely that life really *does begin* at forty! The 'golden years' as implied by advertising agents, do not lie between twenty-three and twenty-eight, for it would seem that their dream candidate is required to possess the head of a fifty-plusser on the shoulders of a twenty-four-year old. This is not, either physically or psychologically – not to mention maturationally – possible, and not always advisable. Rather, employers should take into consideration the *temperaments* of their applicants, for in this way they are far less likely to end up with square pegs in round holes.

Jobs for the – right – boys (and girls)?

There are of course as many variations in temperamental suitability are there are those of occupational, but certain basic rules should be borne in mind concerning

employees' characteristics. Obviously, the two introverted temperaments, the phlegmatics and melancholics,
are best suited to 'closed' working conditions, such as
hospital, office, shop or factory, and so on, and the
more isolated they are in their work the better. On the
other hand, the extroverted cholerics and sanguines feel
drawn to those occupations calling for *outer* initiative,
versatility, flexibility and diversity, in which they are
expected to encounter challenging or interesting situations. Recalling that these two sets of temperaments
are associated with convergent and divergent ways of
thinking respectively, further refinement of this general
plan is possible. (See Chapter 2)

There is an increasing tendency for firms to obtain
the services of graphologists in their search for the
roundest possible peg for the perfectly circular hole.
Some useful indications may undoubtedly be gained
from this. Writing style is acquired by habits which
reflect a person's characteristics; but do not forget that
there is nothing more habitual, by very definition, than
those characteristics which reveal a person's regular
patterns of behaviour, and thereby their temperament.
It is not always easy to match person with job; for later
the situation may change due to circumstances which
cannot be predicted, such as a severe hangover, a tiff
with their partner or sudden disaster in personal relationships, an accident or death in the family, and so on.

Getting down to cases

It is very often the case that people find adopting a
certain role in life reasonably easy, particularly if
they are naturally suited to it. Furthermore, they
often find that they grow with the job, and this is why

it is invariably a good thing to give 'hands-on' experience under guidance as soon as possible, even on a trial basis. Theoretical considerations are all very well, and academic or technical training frequently a necessity, but nevertheless the proof of the pudding is in the eating. Whatever else applies, a thorough study of the temperaments can only be advantageous to employer and employee alike.

Choleric people, being naturally inclined to take the lead in any situation, are well fitted – as a rule – for positions of executive responsibility. They usually possess most useful and desirable qualities for developing into chargehands, foremen, and the various levels of management leading right up to the top. Their powers of initiative, and their instinctive drive and determination, together with their resourcefulness and ability to take in a given situation at a glance, can make them pillars of strength in any organization. Excessive ambition, touchiness, impulsiveness or even aggressiveness may well lead them – and their organization – into difficulties, and this is where an older and wiser individual should be prepared to counsel and admonish as and when necessary during their years of training.

Needless to say, cholerics should recognize that they may need such advice and perhaps correction, even if they do not always welcome it. They often instinctively recognize straightaway that they have overstepped the mark; genuine remorse and regret follows, and this alone may well lead on to self-correction.

People whose main temperament is phlegmatic make very good employees as a rule. They do not mind taking orders, and will carry them out to the letter, methodically and faithfully, if somewhat slowly. They are therefore well suited for skilled work of a repetitive nature, or at least that which involves the principle of regularity and perhaps pre-dictability, for they like to know what is going on, and do not like surprises. Even-tempered, steady and placid, they may safely be left to their own devices, for they are utterly reliable, painstaking and consci-entious. They do not want to be bothered by having to attend to too many details at the same time, and constant distractions from their work tend to make them confused and resentful.

It is as well, too, to make regular enquiries as to their progress/health/contentment, and whether they have anything new to report, for many a phlegmatic worker has observed just how to improve productivity, but remained silent about it. If they make cautious moves in that direction, and an astonished overseer asks why they did not mention it before, they will merely respond: "Well, nobody asked me." Remember that they can't be bothered to volunteer for anything; they prefer to be asked to do something, when they will, out of their usual good nature, and if it is within their capacity, instantly agree to do it. If phlegmatics do require employees, they will probably be few – perhaps as secretaries or other assistants. They are frequently to be found among the ranks of those professional people who work mainly on their own and require few or no helpers, such as law-yers, accountants, dentists and general practitioners, writers, artists, musicians and others whose skills are essentially personal.

Sanguines, being almost certainly divergent in their thinking and extraverted in their behaviour, are always best suited to a pace of work that is fast if not furious, and where there is involvement with people and ongoing events; in short, where the action is. Whether receptionists, insurance salespeople, newshounds, or entertainers and artistes, they, like the cholerics, are on the whole better suited to dealing with people than inanimate objects, and sanguines are particularly talented in this respect. Sociable, talkative and responsive, they are quick to notice everything going on around them, and take appropriate action.

Rather inclined to be carefree, and not always reliable, they may not be very good at punctuality, and not averse to leaving things only partly done or unfinished either. Very often in a hurry or in a self-created mess, they may be untidy in everything else but their personal appearance. Strangers to system, method, and anything in the way of strictly regular routine, and not unknown to bend the rules now and again, typical sanguines feel trapped if too tightly constrained or controlled. They like to feel in every way 'free spirits'; the trouble is that they are too often tempted to turn their liberty into licence. One weakness, which many freely admit to, is the 'gonna' trait: they're 'gonna' do this, they are 'gonna' do that, but alas! there are always yet other things to do. Anything in the way of a priority list or job schedule for completion within a stated time is helpful all round.

Melancholic people tend to be fixed in their ways, as are phlegmatics, but inclined to be more sociable and take more interest in others as individuals. You will find people of this temperament in all the caring professions, for they can be most kind and thoughtful, solicitous and mindful of others. They are extraordinarily capable of experiencing other people's pain and distress as if their own, and feel an urgent wish to alleviate these if they can. Whereas those in the flush of youth would be inclined to be egotistical and demanding, the years of actual or vicarious suffering bring their own reward in the shape of enhanced power of empathy in later life. Naturally, they themselves appreciate tolerance and sympathy from others, and their natural reserve and conservatism tend to render them sensitive to anything in the way of frivolity, flippancy or superficiality in people's behaviour.

Their natural reserve and reluctance to chatter and gossip – that's for sanguines – lead them to choose occupations that involve few or comparatively few individuals, particularly if continuity of association can be maintained, as in a school, hospital or a comparatively small firm or organization. They are seldom drawn to pioneering enterprises, preferring the traditional and well-tried to the innovative, as their need for security is paramount. The typical 'job for life' appeals to them – one with a pension, of course! And if life insurance is thrown in as well – that would be the nearest thing to heaven on earth for our typical melancholics with their 'belt-and-braces' approach to life!

8. Joys and Woes of Compatibility

'Mixed in due proportion'

The Latin origins of the very word 'temperament' imply that which is mixed in due proportion, and it is fortunate for us all that we possess all four temperaments, and not merely one. If this were the case, cholerics would find it impossible to control their quick and violent temper, and would storm around in a permanent state of mania. Sanguines would be like the legendary wild horse which attempted to gallop in all directions at once; they would find every kind of passing attraction impossible to resist, so that the result would be mental instability and collapse into insanity. People whose temperament was one hundred percent phlegmatic would cease to take interest in *anything*, and not bother about themselves or anyone else, gradually deteriorating into a state of permanent imbecility or idiocy. Melancholics whose temperament was not relieved by any of the others would sink deeper and deeper into uncontrollable depression, and pathological melancholia would ensue.

It is said that the heart has reasons that reason does not know, and that love is blind, knows no wrong, and so on. The Irish, wise as ever, maintain that nobody's sweetheart is ugly, and our Caribbean friends claim – and rightly so – that a watertight guarantee of a successful marriage or partnership is simply this: you *must* marry someone who is uglier than yourself! Those who, like Jack Sprat and his wife, whose temperaments complemented one another in concord and harmony, and may be said to be ideally suited in most respects, are the lucky ones. Most human relationships of an intimate nature are for the most part based on personal qualities, attributes and propensities that are *associative* in nature. That is to say, the principles of mutual regard and affection, tolerance and respect, and other factors that are conducive to a rewarding and happy relationship depend on all manner of reciprocal characteristics, and these can be traced to those of the various temperaments.

All this being so, and going by the axiom that forewarned is fore-armed, it is incumbent on me to give some kind of idea as to how the various temperaments are likely to respond to one another at close quarters. We are therefore dealing with a potentially complicated set of factors or parameters; or should I say two sets of temperamental ingredients. The resulting combination in terms of close encounters of whatever kind will be reasonably predictable in the main; but we must never forget that "people are funnier than anybody!" I have fashioned the descriptions and characterizations of these in what follows very much in the manner of verbal caricatures. Various aspects of reality are of course present, but in the main the sketches of both temperamental attributes, and obviously the situations, are deliberately skewed. Our knowledge of the psychology of the temperaments and the predictability of reaction and behaviour notwithstanding, we must always be prepared for the unexpected, or expect that which we have not anticipated, probably for some strange reason lurking somewhere in our complex natures that we are not even conscious of.

There are ten possible combinations of the main

temperaments of two people in partnership, and descriptions of these permutations can only be approximate. Remember that we all have secondary temperaments, and that these must also be taken into consideration. And don't forget, either, that each individual's *personality* plays a very important role as well, not to mention their general health, upbringing and education. The following matchings will serve as a reminder of your own temperamental characteristics. You may not be able actually to *change* your temperament, but at least you should be able to learn how to *handle* it. This is bound to lead to greater and more profound self-knowledge, and that simply cannot be bad.

Choleric/choleric – an explosive mixture

Imagine two volcanoes, at varying stages of quiescence since the last eruption, and you have a fairly clear picture of the general situation, if a somewhat exaggerated one. There is always activity under the surface of typical cholerics, and as they can be very touchy, their 'temperature' must always be watched for the usual danger signs. Their being true extroverts, and divergent in their thinking, we have two strong characters between whom there will always be some degree of tension. If two such people have a similar outlook on life – and this applies to everyone, irrespective of their temperament – this is invariably a strongly mitigating influence; in fact, it can be a very powerful bonding factor, and often is. Bold and brave cholerics have a strength of will envied by those of other temperaments, and they persist in carrying out their intentions with a sometimes foolhardy doggedness and perseverance, even if it kills them, which it may well do – literally. Two cholerics working together must *always* ensure that they are pulling in the same direction – or else!

Both individuals will exhibit the various characteristics we have already discussed, and when it comes to exercising their powers of leadership, for example, the trouble should be taken to ensure that tasks, duties or responsibilities be regularly exchanged, or the person most suited should be 'in charge' at the time. Both partners, being 'blessed' with robust egos, must always be on their guard against the "anything you can do I can do better" syndrome. This kind of thing is plain idiotic, yet rivalries of various kinds can manifest themslves in innumerable ways, some extremely subtle. This is always counter-productive, and can be tiresome, not to say a source of irritation for which cholerics have a low tolerance level anyway. But if they co-operate fully, then mountains can be moved, and Rome built in a day. Excessive impulsiveness, enthusiasm, aggressiveness, optimism and so on should be noted by the other party, and steps taken to cool them out rather than add fire to the flame. A double eruption would give everyone present a spectacular display of fireworks, at which, needless to say, much more heat than light would be generated.

Patience is not the strongest point of either party, and neither is tolerance, for they do not suffer fools gladly. As a rule, however, there is no double eruption, and the person who is not suffering the latest brainstorm or burst of excessive activity should try and recall what they were like during their last bout of it, and call up their fellow-feeling and empathy. Whenever a case of 'choleric collapse' occurs, then this kind of sympathetic behaviour is strongly advisable, even necessary. Any impulse to accord blame, acrimony, criticism, sarcasm, or the incurring of guilt or shame, should be kept well behind the characteristically clenched teeth, for as the saying has it, least said, soonest mended. All their innate kindness and generosity of spirit should be hauled to the surface and exercised instead, for most cholerics have good memories, and are very sensitive beneath that craggy, seemingly hard exterior. They will themselves wait for an opportunity to repay whatever kindness and help has been bestowed on them, so be open-hearted as well as open-handed towards another choleric in distress.

Aggressive behaviour, if not actual violence, should likewise be met with reason and understanding; but if this is not forthcoming, there is only one thing to do. Having been excluded from your plans for the future, they may come creeping – or storming – back, in a state of half-collapse, and then is the time to set out your terms in plain and straightforward language, but curb any tendency towards aggressiveness yourself. You may have to treat such belligerence as one more of many similar learning experiences, and the knowledge as to whether the dissension is worth the candle will emerge sooner or later, and you will both have one more corner knocked off – for that is the story of the lives of all choleric people.

Choleric/sanguine – hot air

Choleric people like to plan for tomorrow, and although keen to get on with the job, they like to be masters of the situation, and are prepared to wait – for a short while. As for sanguines: everything has got to be done – *yesterday*!

Again we have a potentially explosive combination; but generally speaking the choleric partner will have the edge, because sanguines, with their notorious lack of stickability, will tend to lose interest in whatever plans are afoot if they have to wait. However, eager and ambitious as choleric people are, the endless flow of ideas proceeding from the lightning-like sanguine mind will be much appreciated. Sanguine people are capable of weighing up a situation with the speed of light, and the accuracy of their instant judgements, and the rapidity with which they are arrived at, can be impressive. They are more intuitive than cholerics, who make up for this by their grasp of the more practical issues and possibilities. Sanguine people are imaginative and creative, but often lack the courage and grim determination that cholerics are well-known for. Fortunately, perhaps, they are usually too superficial in their approach to enter into any profound discussion or argument, and if they are wise they will not attempt anything in the way of altercation with their choleric partner, but rather come up with yet another brilliant idea to resolve all problems – for the time being, of course!

Individuals of both temperaments are by nature extroverted and divergent in attitude and approach, and this being so, they will have many interests in common. They have the potential for building a rewarding and fulfilling partnership, with excitement, exhilaration and thrills galore an everyday experience – *if* they can stand the pace! There will probably be many a 'patching-up' exercise to carry out, and much in the way of give and take conceded as a matter of course. The tempestuous times that mark their earlier years of association will very likely give way to a period of consolidation and steady progress on all fronts, provided they do not get bored with each other's company. They may not be able to provide sufficient reserves from their *inner* resources to form a firm basis for co-operation in their middle years and beyond. The choleric partner may well deplore the loss of strength and stamina, and the sanguine half of the partnership become increasingly prone to a life of superficiality and emptiness. Both will probably yearn for their lost youth, and should prepare well in advance for their retirement, both mentally and financially.

Choleric/phlegmatic – fire and water

This match seems at first sight to be a sorry one, and doomed from the start, yet this is far from being the case. In the choleric we have an unstable extrovert with divergent ways of approaching everything, and in the phlegmatic we have the complete opposite in every respect, namely a stable introvert with convergent attributes. The scenario is roughly this: either the fire will heat the water to produce steam and energy, or the water will put the fire out. A little reflection will show that this may be no bad thing, provided of course that the situation is appropriate to the action! Now and again, when the choleric partner gets, shall we say *overheated*, then a cooling shower in the shape of typical phlegmatic restraint and caution would not be out of place. The excitability and impulsiveness of the one could with benefit be tempered by the methodical, systematic propensities of the other. Here we have an example of how opposites complement each other, and how well things *could* work.

The question is, as always, whether they *will* work. The patient, plodding phlegmatic, the 'dull as ditch-water' stereotype, with as much get-up-and-go as a well-fed snail, runs the risk of incurring the short-fused choleric's irascibility and intolerance of anything that stands in their way. With practically any other temperament there would be a definite response of some sort, from an equal show of temper from a fellow choleric, a quick exit by a sanguine, or a fit of the sulks by a melancholic. But much of a choleric's bluster and histrionics usually runs off a phlegmatic like water off a duck's back, leaving no impression whatsoever. A sigh that signifies "There he/she goes again," will be the probable reaction, as the patient, long-suffering phlegmatic settles back to wait until the storm blows itself out. Then, a well-chosen, good-humoured remark will most likely take the steam out of the whole situation, and relationships will go back to what passes for normal, with no grudges or recrimina-tions from either side.

The working tolerances on both sides will be worked out reasonably soon, and if there is goodwill between them all should be well in the future.

As mainly active (choleric) and mostly passive (phlegmatic), this match of opposites often results in benefiting both parties. The calm, methodical phleg-matic people may with confidence and trust be left to see to the less exciting aspects of daily life, particularly the shopping and cooking. The dynamic cholerics, with their characteristic energy and drive, may safely be left to get on with everything else that calls for initiative, imagination and enterprise, or that which the other party simply cannot be bothered to get done. In such a matching the secondary temperament could be of considerable importance, but this basic combination could, with sensible and necessary adjustments, be made to work, and work well.

Choleric/melancholic – irresistible force meets immovable object

Here we probably have two parties who love to hate each other. Both parties are unstable, but whereas one is an extrovert and divergent, the other is introvert and convergent; but that is not all. Both have inflated egos, and both are determined to get their own way and assert themselves, the one by sheer force of character and the other by subtle manipulation and other kinds of chicanery. Both will say that they are merely defending themselves from the real or imagined injustices they habitually suffer at the hands of their partner – but it's all a bit of a sham to friends and observers, who most likely consider them to be a pair of sillies. Why did they ever pair up in the first place? will be their question!

Well, just imagine the scenario – somewhat exaggerated, of course. In the red corner we have a born leader, a go-getter, a ball of fire – someone who *will* get their own way, in their own way, come hell or high water – regardless. In the blue corner we have someone who *will* get their way – also regardless; but they, stubborn if quiet with it, are nevertheless clever thinkers and superb strategists. They have to be! Of course, they would not openly admit all this, but every day sees battle stations – wit versus wiles – in a kind of David and Goliath stand-off.

There must be more than this to any choleric/melancholic relationship, and naturally there is. The soulful, serious, retiring and ever-devoted melancholic lady of the house, who slaves away in factory or office, who gives up her time and energy to earn, to please, to sacrifice herself even, all because of her undying love and affection for her nearest and dearest – surely all this practical regard deserves some kind of recognition. Her voice breaks with emotion, and a handkerchief or tissue appears as if from nowhere. A sigh is followed by a sniff, and the sniff by a sigh; the uplifted eyes are moist and red. She has given up everything for her loved one; body, soul – *everything*. Her sufferings show through now and again, and she apologises for it, but what they do reveal is the merest, minutest fraction of what she feels deep in her heart. She lies awake at night, silent in her anguish, not disturbing her darling partner for a second in spite of it; but all the while she is aching to empty her soul of the pain and misery that is hers. But no, she does not wish her beloved to suffer as she does – not now, not tomorrow, not *ever*!

Her choleric partner, strong and resourceful, hard-working and industrious, devoted and dedicated, surveys the heart-rending scene. How dependent this frail, slight, delicate and relatively uncomplaining(!), darling woman, for whom he had so gladly and willingly given up so much – how reliant she really was on him. Working unceasingly for ever higher qualifications, and to impress his boss by taking on far more work than most of his colleagues – had he not shown ambition, grit and determination, perseverance, tenacity and endurance? True, she was a sympathetic listener when he got in late, tired and weary after a long day at work – and yet more to do before bedtime – telling him reluctantly (!) of those awful people in the office, whom she knew were complaining about her attacks of migraine behind her back, accusing her of feigning them. Yes, he knew about her frequent headaches, poor darling. As she is always telling him, self-denial is good for the soul, so he would have to try it. There was only one thing to do, of course; and that was to work even harder, gain even greater recognition from his boss, and prove that he really deserves a seat on the board. Then she would be able to give up her work, feel better, happier, less tense and out of sorts. Her bouts of depression would disappear as a result, and she would then recover the former health and high spirits which she had had when they met...

Sanguine/sanguine – What's new, Pussycat?

What else but the term 'airy-fairy' could come to mind in view of this relationship? We have already mentioned that theirs is the element of Air, and so a vision of two butterflies cavorting amongst the flowers presents itself. After all, they both have 'butterfly minds', and are borne on the wings of the wind and flit unceasingly from idea to idea – and airy-fairy ones for the most part, need I add! So everything has got to be all sweetness and light, has it not?

Well, er – no, not exactly. Nothing is perfect in this world, though many a sanguine person may harbour the cosy notion that maybe – only maybe, of course – they are just that little bit more perfect than anyone else. Tom is domineering and over-bearing; Dick's interests extend no further than creature comforts and working out what and when the next meal is; Harry is a bag of misery and sulks all the time, so that leaves me – good-looking, charming, lively, witty, sociable, carefree. So if you have two of us, by the laws of arithmetic that means a doubling of all these super qualities, and heaven too. Right? Well, er – no, not exactly. Don't you ever get a teeny-weeny bit bored with – dare I say it – each other's company sometimes? You don't wish to discuss that?

And so we could go on. For what could disturb this perfect harmony but that two people have different ideas at the same time, the same ideas at different times, or different ideas at different times, but never the same ideas at the same time? A two-member mutual admiration society hardly leaves much room for manoeuvre. When two whirlwinds come together, anything can happen, and this is of course the great question mark that is continuously hanging over this partnership of two. Both being volatile, mercurial, inconstant, erratic, capricious, irresolute and variable, our unpredictable and ever-changeable couple will, whatever else, have a pretty hard time of it – and all of their own making. Their very temperament makes this a certainty.

According to the *secondary* temperament each possesses, there may not only be many disagreements or rows as a matter of course, but also fumings and tantrums, moping and pouting, sulks and heavy silences, aggressiveness and truculence, indifference and apathy – and we have met all these characteristics in previous pages.

Of course there will be good times too, and with increasing years, in both chronological as well as maturational terms, these should become more and more frequent. Gradually, to their natural charm will be added the qualities of grace and poise, polish and refinement, even composure and dignity. Retaining their essential liveliness and vivacity, they will bestow their gifts of sociability and sensitivity to the feelings and needs of others, on all and sundry. They will enliven every place where people gather, their company will be sought, and they will be popular in the best sense of the word. Perhaps the most difficult temperament to handle, whether one's own or of others, particularly if they are near and dear, sanguinity can be as much a blessing as a burden.

Sanguine people are extroverted and divergent; they are almost totally outwardly turned, and their inner resources are often poorly developed. By way of compensation, they address themselves one-sidedly to the demands and attractions of the outside world, unsatisfactory as these may well prove in the long run. This means that their inner life is, as it were, starved and deprived of the benefits to be gained from quiet reflection on their experiences and pondering the meaning of life in general, not to mention its specific problems. The only stable feature of people of sanguine temperament is their fundamental instability, and clearly, this is why the complementary characteristics contributed by their secondary temperament is of such vital significance and importance. Moreover, this is why it is almost impossible to make any definite comments about this particular combination. On the principle of *compatibility by reason of associative qualities*, and these qualities being what they are, namely as variable as the very air itself, the path of progress may well be a difficult one, but almost certainly a rewarding one.

Sanguine/phlegmatic – bubbles

It might be an exaggeration to claim that this pair will spend most of their time blowing "pretty bubbles in the air", but nevertheless we have the potential for a very compatible partnership here. They are both *stable* in their basic structure and conformation: the sanguines in that their very instability is a constant factor, and the phlegmatics are more stable in every way, in terms of temperament, than any other category. In other respects they are polar opposites: sanguines are extroverted and divergent, whereas phlegmatics are introverted and convergent. Furthermore, they are very much concerned with what is going on in the *present* in terms of time: sanguine people are concerned rather with considerations of a psychological or mental nature, whereas phlegmatic people involve themselves rather with what is solid and material.

Opposite in practically every respect to phlegmatics then, sanguine people would do well to consider choosing a partner who is one. The slow, steady, patient, methodical phlegmatic – especially if male – is capable of functioning as a very effective counterbalance to his sanguine partner, whose feet hardly ever touch the ground! She can float away on the clouds of fancy and fantasy with abandon, revelling in extravagant imaginings of all kinds, but knowing full well that her steadfast and reliable, if somewhat dull and bemused partner, will see her safely back to earth once more. She may fondly imagine that he is indulgent towards her in particular, and that the reason why he tolerates her waywardness in certain directions is on account of his rock-steady devotion to her, and this may well be true.

But she should also stop and consider, perhaps, just why he *is* so tolerant and accepting, lenient and understanding, if she wishes to stir his porridge-like mentality. The truth is that so much, so very, very much of what goes on around him simply passes him by; he notices only those elements of his surroundings that he wishes to, for he is capable of 'switching off' at will – or even sleeping at will! Lively and wide-awake, interested in everything and with thoughts racing, she may pause to spare him a tender thought, and even give him an affectionate peck as she whistles past him, relaxed and imperturbable in his favourite armchair. She never misses a trick, of course, and wonders how her poor darling ever manages to put up with her skittish ways.

Invariably forbearing and uncomplaining, he overlooks her sanguine vagaries, taking all her moods and trivialities in his stride, knowing full well that sooner or later she will return to some degree of normality!

He for the most part chooses what to notice and what not to, taking care to separate the permanent from the transitory, the really important from the insignificant. The family finances are best left to him, for she knows only too well that the cheque book and credit cards belong to his domain. If she seeks to liven things up by acquiring a new dress or slinky nightwear, she may need all her feminine wiles, and in time she will learn just how to handle him. But if she senses that he is about to dig his heels in, she knows that she had better back off; for once he has made up his mind about anything, that's that! Not that he is unreasonable, and not ready to listen to a serious proposition; on the contrary, he is usually generous and openhanded if the money is there – and if he lingers and shuffles around at the delicatessen counter during the weekly shopping trip, naturally she takes the hint.

Of course, a sanguine male partner would get tired of hanging around such an attractive spot, while his phlegmatic counterpart feasts her eyes on the expanse of delectables, knowing he will have time to dash around to the wines and spirits department to see what catches his eye. He will get back to find her slow and studied deliberations, but he knows better than to interrupt, knowing full well that she will consider his tastes as well as her own, and that he can confidently look forward to next week's mealtimes with the customary enthusiasm and gusto. Outgoing and amiable as he may be, she knows that she may have reasonable grounds for suspicion if he has *too* many evenings out with the boys, playing tennis or golf, or whatever.

Most things considered, our seemingly incompatible couple may be seen to balance each other out quite well. The most likely source of friction and dissension between them will be excessive pigheadedness over apparently small matters on the part of the phlegmatic partner, and immoderate behaviour on the part of the sanguine partner; and he will know when that moment arrives, because even a worm will turn when sufficiently provoked. If he cannot or will not read the signs, then it will certainly be the worse for him! But sanguine people are very perceptive, sensitive and responsive, and compassion and genuine fellow-feeling and concern for others are generally to be found in their make-up. As always, the secondary temperaments play a large part in any association; and in the case we have been discussing, the worst of all possible worlds would result, perhaps, if the sanguine partner was afflicted with a melancholic streak, and the phlegmatic partner with choleric one.

Sanguine/melancholic – chalk and cheese

Here we have an association of opposites in practically every respect. Sanguine extraversion and divergent ways of looking at things is ranged alongside – but in many ways against, of course – melancholic introversion and convergent habits of thinking. However lacking in associative characteristics, this pair have much to gain from their very polarities. The flighty, capricious, whimsical sanguine could certainly find balance in the steady, serious, reserved melancholic, and here again the nature of the secondary temperaments of both is of paramount importance.

Problems would certainly arise if, say, the melancholic partner stubbornly refused to be torn away from the book he or she was halfway through, simply because the sanguine's favourite group happened to be performing in the next town. The latter flounces out in a fit of pique, and after thoroughly enjoying the concert in spite of their tiff, skitters into the house at almost midnight, bursting with enthusiasm and excitement and brimming over with goodwill, simply unable to wait for a second to tell the former all about it – only to find the living room empty, and the bedroom door locked. Repeated impassioned pleas to open it are met with audible sobs or stony silence, and so the bed in the spare room is furiously and resentfully retired to. At breakfast-time next morning, predictably enough, our melancholic, if appearing at all, would be either tearful or grumpy. Our sanguine, however piqued and offended, is willing to forgive and forget for the sake of harmony and concord – and that cosy double bed. That evening would see signs of thaw, most likely; the sanguine partner being extra solicitous and considerate, and the melancholic one coy and unusually anxious – but this time to please, perhaps.

The kind of wearing, nerve-wracking manoeuvring in a tense, prickly atmosphere that I have just characterized will inevitably occur from time to time, at least until a few corners have been knocked off, negotiations completed, and contentment restored. Of course, many couples think the joys of making up are worth the row that caused the rift, but it can nevertheless be a chancy, if not actually dangerous, scenario. The sanguine partner, sick, tired and thoroughly fed up with the vagaries of their melancholic lover, might well consider taking flight from the nuptual nest. The melancholic partner, also sick, tired and thoroughly fed up with the vagaries of their sanguine lover, might well consider recourse to legal proceedings.

Both sanguines and melancholics live to a very great extent on their nerves; and characteristically enough, this is revealed in terms of behavioural problems and personal problems respectively. The sanguines, being active, impulsive and even devil-may-care, are more likely to take refuge in outer events, and to take their chance by moving away. The melancholics, fixed and rigid in their thinking and general attitudes, would rather seek to maintain their security in the home, being apprehensive, even fearful, of what could await them in the unknown outside world. So it is largely a matter of courage versus apprehension, adventurousness versus reserve, responsiveness versus obdurateness, flexibility versus rigidity, and optimism and ever-springing hope versus pessimism and unrelievable despair.

Sanguines can be difficult in their particular ways, just as melancholics can be perverse in theirs; and often, it must be said, there will be very little common ground on which they can meet. We are therefore back to the old question of the leopard changing its spots, and there seems to be little likelihood of that in the case of either party. As ever the two factors, represented by the secondary temperament on the one hand, and the passage of time on the other, need to be borne in mind and taken into account. This is necessary for the maturing and development of the characteristics conferred by both their temperaments, and they can do little more than hope that their particular mixtures come "in due proportion" and so facilitate their continuing happy and successful partnership.

Phlegmatic/phlegmatic – Tweedledum and Tweedledee: a rare pair

The formula for this merger is: $\dfrac{\text{inertia}}{\text{inertia}} = \text{inertia}$

because according to the laws of nature like can only *beget* like!

They are both stable, introverted and convergent, and so exhibit a certain lack of balance in some respects, although, as mentioned elsewhere (p. 47) they possess the compensating attribute of being able to find their own level, as fluids do. This probably accounts for the terms people apply to phlegmatics in general: even-tempered, level-headed, flat-footed, perhaps – but never 'flat spin'!

Joking apart, this partnership promises to be the most stable one conceivable; and two such individuals would make excellent subjects for a real 'still life' picture. At school they soon get used to being called 'fatty', 'porky', 'piggy' and so on – but do they care? Only if the victim possesses the choleric temperament as the subordinate one, in which case the name-caller had better watch it! But by long tradition such roly-polies, the short and fat people, are jolly withal, so it would be a mistake to consider phlegmatics to be genuinely dull – they merely give that impression. Sometimes this suits them, for then people don't bother them, pester them, harass them, for this they do not like. Never 'keep on' at them, and beware arguments!

Our couple know all this of course, so actual communication between the two is likely to be minimal. Naturally, telepathy cannot be entirely ruled out, especially if their association is a long-standing one.

When passivity is reinforced by passivity, the result will be negative, for two minuses do not make a plus in the arithmetic of Phlegmatica. Their main hope lies in the kind of secondary temperament they each possess. If it is relieved by the sanguine, as it very often is, then a delightful rhythm will probably generate itself, a kind of in-breathing and out-breathing, reflected in disinterest/interest, unsociability/sociability, talkativeness/taciturnity, passivity/activity and so on. If both partners are similarly blessed, so much the better. The same prospect would probably apply if they both have choleric as their main supporting temperament.

If the secondary temperament of one or both is melancholic, the situation will certainly be rendered more interesting, whatever else. As well as the intense inwardness of the easy-going stability of the phlegmatic, there will be the appreciable self-centredness contributed by the melancholic temperament. This may well result in a sort of gloomy stubbornness, which will not merely apply to the owner of this particular mixture in his or her refusal to disclose where the new packet of chocolate biscuits has been cached. The same kind of thinking will be applied to all sorts of "what's-yours-is-mine" situations, and the pure phlegmatic or phlegmatic/sanguine will probably give way – up to a certain point, of course – time after time after time.

Because of their apparent placidity – for still waters really do run deep – many people make the mistake of regarding phlegmatic people as 'walk-overs'. Again, the two of them would know this too, and both be fore-armed. They would scarcely go to the trouble of attempting to chagrin each other – it simply isn't worth it. If they are going shopping, the decision as to where to go will probably be made by the first to speak, for the other would be glad that he/she has been relieved of the tremendous burden of having to take a decision on the matter.

Great minds think alike – but then, fools never differ; and the one thing they would certainly agree on would be the time for the next meal, and probably the one after that.

Their home would of course be very cosy and comfortable, and carry that unmistakable air of being lived in. It will be only reasonably tidy, the furniture and furnishing solid and durable, with no pretences in the way of the fashionable. Here live real home-makers, for home is where they like to spend their time.

Visitors are always welcome, but moreso if they have announced their intentions to come along well in advance. A welcome opportunity would thereby be provided for the partaking of one or two extra chocolate biscuits without suffering a single pang of conscience on the part of either of our phlegmatic home-birds. The conversation may well be one-sided, but any issue raised would have to be very contentious before the hackles of either of our very special couple would be raised, not to mention their voices. However, watch for such signs as barely audible sighs, shuffling of feet and frequent watch-watching, especially if the hour is late; bedtime routines must in no way be intruded upon.

Phlegmatic/melancholic –
"There's a hole in my bucket"

This is another unlikely match: stable introvert and unstable introvert, the first indifferent and unconcerned, and the second egotistical and pessimistic. Prospects are not very favourable, so I intend to make short work of this particular scenario. Neither knows the meaning of excitement, enthusiasm and sociability; what they do know is their own private world which they keep hidden from each other as well as everyone else, unless they have private reasons for not so doing. It is very likely that an unequal struggle will ensue, perhaps not so much at the conscious level as the unconscious. The self-centred, demanding and self-seeking melancholic will set about taking over the easy-going, patient and self-effacing phlegmatic by stealth, and make a slave of him or her.

This of course is the starkest sort of scenario imaginable, but it is nevertheless characteristic of the basic situation. Here again, the secondary temperaments of both will be of crucial importance, and enough has been said for you to exercise your imagination in this direction. But secondary temperaments are that by definition, and the primary ones are bound to show through strongly, especially if the opportunity arises for manipulation, whether subtle or blatant, particularly on the part of the melancholic partner. The dismal fact is that we are, each single one of us, fundamentally selfish in our dealings with our fellows: we are all egotists, and we all have, in varying degrees, an eye for the main chance. Number One always comes first, and this is undeniable in terms of number and general human behaviour.

Imagine then, if you will, a melancholic male partner whose counterpart is phlegmatic. He, peevish, cantankerous and petulant at worst, and grudging, moody and anxious at best, is only rarely inclined to go out of his way to bring out the best in people, including his nearest and dearest, perhaps. She, misguidedly making attempts to please him by plying him with all kinds of goodies, favours, and other gestures of goodwill, may learn, perhaps too late, that she may as well save herself the trouble. Indifference, perhaps the greatest weakness of the phlegmatic, is likely to set in, and she will tend more and more to go her own way and please herself; after all, do what she will or might, all she gets back is criticism, unwanted advice, and hurtful remarks. Usually slow to anger and not easily provoked, her resentment will nevertheless build, and her prevailing mood of calm and self-control become thin and brittle.

The scene is now set for impending disaster. She, sensitive, long-suffering and even-tempered for the most part, and having gone out of her way to please in every respect, finds that even her very best efforts are not good enough. He, pressing for every advantage that he possibly can in typical egotistical fashion, succeeds in driving her into a corner from which she feels she cannot escape. She has been made to feel inadequate, inefficient, and perhaps even a failure, and sooner or later she will, like Spadge in Laurie Lee's *Cider with Rosie*, "have had enough". The consequence could well be explosive, and the formerly amiable, good-natured and gentle woman transmogrified into a violent, even murderous, brute. This kind of situation is of course somewhat melodramatic, but is perfectly feasible nonetheless; for it is in such circumstances that many a 'crime of passion' has come about.

It is unlikely that the phlegmatic partner would deliberately set out to inflict any hurt, provoke any row, or in any way deliberately to plot her own selfish advantage. Phlegmatics hate to be upset, preferring to remain on an even keel in a flat calm. Unpleasantness of whatever kind is abhorrent to them, and they will go to endless trouble to avoid it; they will never rock the boat unless very severely provoked. As for her melancholic opposite number: he may well be piqued because of her seeming indifference towards him, for his ego needs to be constantly nurtured and cherished. If this solicitous behaviour is not forthcoming he may even feel deprived and neglected, or perhaps even rejected. The scenario described earlier, seen from his strictly limited point of view, is understandably irritating. But a melancholic's irritation threshold is not very high as a rule, and his acquisitive propensities would urge him to obtain what he can whilst he can. He would almost certainly turn more and more inward, nursing real – or more likely imagined – grudges and resentments, turning them over and over in his mind, fostering them and multiplying them.

Depression would ensue sooner or later, for he would be unable to bring about any kind of change. His phlegmatic partner, impassive and ostensibly becoming more and more remote, immovable in her reluctance to change her ways, is perceived by him as a threat to his own sense of security. He feels uneasy, suspicious, anxious. How did it all start? Why is she so undemonstrative? What is she plotting? What are her ulterior motives? Is she really to be trusted? And so the self-torment goes on and on. When she finally does blow her top, he is surprised and shocked, not realizing that he, all the while, has been tormenting her...

Melancholic/melancholic – blue moons

Of all combinations in terms of compatibilty, this is certainly one of the most interesting. Here we have two basically introverted, convergent, unstable characters, who will almost certainly experience much in the way of personal difficulties. Inevitably, these will manifest as *inter-personal* complications, and the closer the relationship the greater these are likely to be because each harbours similar notions; that he or she suffers afflictions more keenly than anyone else could possibly realise or understand. Melancholics are as a result more sensitive, more sympathetic, more compassionate and more tender towards others than are people possessing other temperaments. Deep down in their hearts and souls melancholics know this. Unfortunately, however, difficulties arise when they also expect everyone else to possess such qualities, and extend these virtues to them, and they are sadly disappointed when their expectations are not met.

This may be regarded as something of an over-statement. However, such attitudes will not be applied in 'blanket' fashion, more likely manifesting themselves in piecemeal fashion, unevenly and fragmentedly according to whatever circumstances or situations prevail at the time. For example, they will go to enormous trouble and inconvenience to alleviate the sufferings of the little old lady across the road, whilst neglecting their nearest and dearest at home. The profuse thanks for their kindnesses, the thankful sighs, grateful looks and admiring comments praising their deeds of self-denial, are accepted as a matter of course, and serve to confirm that they themselves are indeed very special people, and their ego becomes pervaded with a cosy glow.

Self-satisfaction and inner pride are included among the less attractive qualities of melancholics. They secretly love to be the centre of attention, and if challenged they would strenuously deny this; but as they are not usually ostentatious and over-demanding about it – at least to start with – their 'admirers' often overlook this trait. Our smug, self-satisfied, self-right-eous, superior melancholic suffers from the delusion that they actually *deserve* the ministrations of others, and accept them as of right, and frequently without a word of thanks.

If they are in a blue mood or brown study, limp, listless and spent, they may find it difficult to snap out of it and get the evening meal ready, go to work in the morning, or put themselves out in any way. They feel that their family and friends should show them solici-tude and sympathy, should minister to them as a kind of duty – it is, after all, what they *should* do.

So when we have the situation of two melancholics in close partnership, there are numerous possible scenarios, ranging from a two-person mutual admi-ration society to a pair of miserable, crabby, endlessly complaining, griping, grousing, criticizing, disap-proving ingrates. Happily – if I dare employ such a word in this context – these represent extremes, and as ever there are mitigating influences in the shape of their secondary temperaments. What must always be remembered is that melancholics are, perhaps more than people of other temperaments, inclined to be blind to their own faults. It is important to realize that they are, however unapparent this may be to them,

egotistic; what they crave for incessantly is understanding and solicitude. Their need for security is so
crucial that they feel the need to convince themselves
in many and various ways that they really are safe
from all the evils in the world.

The capacity for self-torment is considerable. It is as
though they are not truly fulfilling themselves unless
they are suffering in some way or other. A melancholic
couple would therefore tend, at various times, to suffer
with each other, for each other; they will, I grieve to add,
scarcely avoid circumstances in which they will torment
each other. There seems a perverse yearning to suffer;
and I would go as far as to say that in some severer cases
it is a matter of actually feeling guilty if they are not
allowed to suffer! Visited by affliction, they wallow in it!
Like the cartoon figure of the typical Britisher at the
seaside on a wet Bank Holiday, they are determined to
enjoy themselves, even if it means suffering for the
pleasure of it!

Whether consciously or unconsciously, they will
contribute to each other's woes and sorrows; they will
suffer affliction, distress and even torment together,
and each for the other, each by the other's actions.
It will be largely up to them as to whether old age will
be their friend. The next day may be sadder than the
day before, but at least they will be wiser, and this
wisdom they are well fitted to pass on to the up and
coming generation. In the long run the consequences
will include blessings and individual betterment. As a
result of their tribulations they will almost certainly
become nobler personalities, and their characters will
develop to the benefit of both themselves and the world.

9. LOVE –
That's Why We're Here!

In a certain sense, the attributes typical of our particular temperament can be likened, so to speak, to psychological 'cards' that we have been dealt, and which we have little option but to 'play' in the game of human relationships and social interactions generally. At this point the intriguing question arises – if it hasn't arisen before now – how is it that we have been dealt the particular temperamental and characteristic cards that we find ourselves with? Is it due to chance or predetermination, fate or fortune, luck, providence or whatever? How do we become what we were at birth, and are now?

Scientists talk learnedly about genes, chromosomes, chains of DNA and suchlike, which seem to determine our behaviour. According to them, it is such as these that make up a kind of 'blue-print', a chart or pre-arranged plan of our constitution as human beings. Nature is anything but simple, and there is no simple answer to the question of how we come to be what we are.

If scientists tell us that we are no more and no less than what our genes oblige us to be, then they are being simplistic. They know as well as we do that although *heredity* is a major factor in determining the constitution of each one of us, it is by no means the whole story. If this were the case, children of the same parents would all be alike as so many peas, and this we know they certainly are not!

Clever as modern scientists undoubtedly are, they nevertheless seem to be bedazzled by their own achievements in the realm of technology. They seem to seek to explain everything to do with Nature – and after all we must not forget that we *are* part of it – in terms of technology. Examples of this are comparing the human brain with a highly complicated computer of advanced design, our nervous system as an intricate telegraphic network, our digestive organization as one of combustion, our heart as a pump, and so on. In effect, we human beings have been reduced to the status of animated machines which have to be kept serviced by the use of the appropriate drugs, and in good repair by having our diseased organs replaced by so-called spare-part surgery. Terms such as biotechnology and genetic engineering are everyday terms. In other words, we consist, according to some scientists, of nothing else but a body, an extraordinarily complex mechanism of living matter – but a mechanism all the same.

But what of soul and spirit (if any)?

Terms such as soul and spirit have all but died out, for they are no longer meaningful; but there was a time when they did mean something, and represented realities. However, theologians and psychologists between them have succeeded in devaluing both to the point of meaninglessness. Whatever feelings we have are now regarded as being based entirely on bodily processes, and our highest ideals as arising from certain quirky goings-on in the crinkles of our cerebrum. Even life itself is widely believed to arise from organic matter like a flame from its candle, liable to be snuffed out at any time – to be gone for ever.

Such notions as these belong strictly to modern times. It is common experience, however, that we all inhabit two worlds: one, our inner world comprising our thoughts and feelings, is invisible and intangible, private, hidden, and undetectable by any of our five bodily sense organs; and another, the outer world which is discernible by means of our senses, that is visible, tangible and public, and there for all to share.

However, the further we go back into history, the more we find that the unseen phenomena of Nature were not only just as real to people, right up to the Middle Ages, as the visible, but were regarded as representing true reality, whereas what was visible was considered as merely instrumental to, and contingent on, this reality. In other words, these two worlds were seen as representative of the *spirit* on the one hand, and *matter* on the other. Our ancestors believed that matter was spirit 'at rest', and thus as having its origin in the unseen worlds beyond reach of the senses. In effect, spirit and matter were essentially the same.

That was roughly the picture as regards Nature in general. As far as *human* nature was concerned, our forefathers believed that they maintained their existence in both worlds: the intransient, unchanging world of spirit, and the transient, changeable world of matter. From this it was easily deducible that everything of a spiritual nature was everlasting, and as such not subject to decay and death, in contrast to everything of a material nature, which was. From this point of view, therefore, human beings were justified in regarding themselves as comprising two main elements: their spirit, deathless and immortal, and their material body, which was mortal. Nowadays, people have no choice but accept the latter proposition even if they do not accept the former!

So far we have accounted for spirit and body; the *soul* element was considered to arise from the interaction between the spirit 'from above', and matter 'from below'. Of course, not everyone will go along with these observations and propositions, considering, perhaps, that each one of us is a 'product' of our parents, inheriting their genes in various proportions. Thus equipped, we are then launched into the world, to be subjected to whatever influences our upbringing and general socialization, education and training expose us to.

Earlier on I mentioned that whatever main temperament, together with its various basic attributes, we are 'dealt' is more or less what we acquire almost before birth. This implies that there is an certain lack of choice available to us in being landed with one or other main temperament. The problem arises: is it a matter of chance or of choice? Has the particular temperament we possess been as it were forced on us, and are we victims of the genetic cards we have been dealt? Have we been led blindly into the temperamental trap we find ourselves in by the mere play of chance?

The materialistically inclined reader may well think so; but many others – the majority, perhaps – may think that, well, there's something not quite right with being made mere playthings of chance, victims of circumstances, or similar. Lingering feelings of unease are often the result, and many people start to blame God, or the Devil, their bad luck, their parents or whoever or whatever. Why should they – how could they – blame themselves, or even thank themselves, for their own particular predicament? These kinds of reflections do not make for a serene or settled mind, and for many the problems remain.

Is the notion of reincarnation so very weird?

More people in the world than not hold the belief that their present life is one of many; that they have lived through many incarnations, and will live through many more. This notion is not particularly widespread in the West, but it must be said that it is becoming accepted as sound and reasonable by more and more people. Matter is destructible, whereas spirit is not; and it could be argued from this that if human beings are comprised of *both* these principles and not merely the material, then some kind of existence after death – and by implication before birth also – is a certainty rather than a mere belief. People who believe in life after death must, by reason of sheer logic, believe in life before birth: deathlessness must necessarily be complemented by birthlessness. The word so sorely lacking in the vocabularies of so many languages is that which yields the concept of *birthlessness*, for immortality is generally understood in the very limited sense of *deathlessness*. It seems remarkable that the notion of *pre-natal* existence of the human 'spirit' or 'soul' is so widely disregarded throughout the Western world, whereas its *post-mortem* existence is quite commonly accepted as belief or even fact in many other parts. Obviously, this appeals to the egotism in people, because the desire to continue to exist after death is very strong. A 'soul' – or any other entity for that matter – if once understood to possess the attributes of eternity, must be understood to have possessed them eternally; the argument is irrefutable. Anyone who believes in life after death must, in order to preserve the necessary logic involved, believe in its obverse, namely life before birth. Accordingly, equally lacking is a word approximating to *unbornness*; that is to say, a state of pre-existence. If the whole concept of immortality is to be taken seriously, the words *birthlessness* and *deathlessness* must be regarded equally so. The inescapable consequence to these considerations is the concept of *re-incarnation*, or repeated earthly embodiments. But as in other controversial or emotive situations, "you pays yer money and takes yer choice". This is not the place to launch into lengthy discussion about the pros and cons of reincarnation and its twin companion – karma or self-created destiny, intriguing though that may be.

Interestingly enough, when heredity is discussed, it is usually with implications that we are what our parents have made us, temperaments and all. But the picture may well be much, much more complicated than that. Many reincarnationists maintain that we all *choose* our parents long before birth, and by inference that which we lumber ourselves with by way of temperament. So, in the last resort, they insist, we have only ourselves to thank for what we are when we find ourselves born into such and such a family and into whatever race, colour or creed. The philosopher, educationist and social scientist Rudolf Steiner, whose little book *The Four Temperaments* is thoroughly recommended, put the whole matter of temperament in a nutshell:

> There is indeed an intermediary between what is brought over from earlier lives on earth and what is provided by heredity. This intermediary has more universal qualities provided by family, nation and race, but is at the same time capable of individualization. That which stands between the line of heredity and the individuality is expressed in the word *temperament*.[1]

Our fourfold nature

We have already established that four temperaments will not 'go' into three bodily types; and this helps to show that Nature's ways are far from simple, for the further we seek the more of her basic principles are revealed to us. The question arises: does the ancient tradition of our comprising body, soul and spirit fit the three somatotypes I discuss in detail in Appendix II: Somatotype comes from the Greek and means *body type*. The answer seems to be that they do not – that we are *fourfold* in our essential being.

Earlier on (pp. 102-103) we discussed the notion of our inhabiting two worlds – our inner, private world of thoughts and feelings, and the outer, public world of material things. These worlds are of course in polar opposition to one another, and it is the realisation of this that gave rise to the widespread notion and belief that we human beings are correspondingly *twofold* in our constitution. This is borne out by the extensively held tenet that we consist of body and soul only, and it was necessary to point out the muddled thinking that surrounds these terms. But there is a strong case for arguing that the *soul* arises as a result of the interaction between the two polar opposites represented in our *spirit* and our *body*. In this model the soul is vitally involved with these two opposing factors, being influenced by both and influencing both.

Now it could be postulated that, in consideration of our four temperaments, the attributes of which have been examined from various standpoints already, they could with justification be split into two sets of two. That is to say, two may be regarded as exhibiting factors of a *spiritual* nature, and two expressive of our *bodily* nature.

The following chart will help to make this clear: (see also page 13)

Bodily nature	{Phlegmatic } {Melancholic }	introverted, passive (inner world concerns)
Spiritual nature	{Sanguine } {Choleric }	extroverted, active (outer world concerns)

This is yet another way of looking at the main temperaments and their attributes and connections, which contributes to a deeper understanding and appreciation of the human condition.

As mentioned in Chapter 1, the four temperaments are by tradition linked with the four elements of Ancient Greek science.

Also closely associated with these elements was the notion that human beings possess not only a physical body of more or less solid flesh and bone, which is visible and tangible, but also no fewer than three more 'bodies' or 'vehicles', principles which are invisible and intangible, and not in any way accessible by means of our traditional five senses:

Element	Principle	Temperament
Fire	Ego (or 'I')	Choleric
Air	Astral body	Sanguine
Water	Etheric body	Phlegmatic
Earth	Physical body	Melancholic

Of these four, as might be expected, the heaviest and most dense is the vehicle composed of the very stuff of the earth itself – the 'dust' of the biblical story of Creation. This must be so, for all our nutriments originate in the soil beneath our feet, and are absorbed by means of the food we eat, whether directly of plant origin or indirectly by way of meat and various other animal products. This is the only 'body' recognized by modern materialistic science, as mentioned earlier. It is no coincidence that melancholic individuals feel the sheer weight of their physical body more than people of other temperaments. Their actions are inclined to be slower, their features long and downdrawn, and their limbs longer and less controllable, and their whole demeanour suggestive of being especially under the influence of *gravity*. It is just as if they are carrying the whole world on their shoulders.

Phlegmatic folk are those in whom the influences of their *etheric* body are most dominant. Another equally suitable term for this principle would be 'life-body' or 'formative-forces-body'. Itself invisible, it nevertheless makes its presence plainly evident by the manner in which the form and substance of the physical-material or 'earthly' body is maintained and regenerated. Obviously, the chemical substances of which the earthly body is made are not in any way *alive*; they possess no vitality of their own. Rather, it is the etheric body which takes up these substances in an anabolic or constructive way, and which is responsible for the powers of growth and reproduction that every living organism possesses. In fact, its main function is that of organizing and constructing; every living *organism* must by definition have an etheric body. When the etheric principle departs from any organism, what we call death ensues, and all its chemical components return to the earth from whence they came.

The supreme illustration of the co-existence and co-operation of the physical and etheric bodies is found in all members of the plant kingdom, all of which fulfil the three main criteria applicable: organization of matter, and growth and reproduction.

How can the notion of predominance of the etheric forces in a phlegmatic individual be substantiated? There is scarcely a single person whose main temperament is that of phlegmatic who does not live – luxuriate, even – in their digestive juices and body fluids in general. If melancholics are best characterized by their heightened experience of the heaviest components of their body, namely their bones, then phlegmatics may be said to exist mainly in the various secretions of their glandular systems, and it need hardly be pointed out that these are fluid in their consistency, thus qualifying in terms of Greek science as *water*. It is small wonder that cholerics and others get hot under the collar – or rapidly lose interest in – such a temperament when suffering the porcine in shape, and pig-headed by nature, phlegmatic.

The element of *air* is associated with our third 'body' or principle, namely the 'astral' or 'sentient' body, so called because it is traditionally the vehicle for our feelings. Everything we experience as love or hate, like and dislike, and sympathy and antipathy generally, we owe to our astral body. Its hallmark is the possession by any organism of a nervous system and the experiencing of *consciousness*; and this is characteristic of not only ourselves but the whole of the animal kingdom. Plants do not have a nervous system nor any kind of sense organ, and so do not experience any kind of feeling or consciousness.

It is not difficult to discern the connections between the enhanced consciousness of the typical sanguine person and the astral principle. Of all people, sanguine individuals are prone to nervousness and restlessness, endlessly searching for different experiences. They could almost be described as hyper-conscious, noticing everything that goes on around them with bird-like intensity, whereas our slow, methodical, inwardly turned phlegmatics allow events to wash over them, taking in only what they choose to and not bothering at all with what might attract the immediate attention and (usually passing) interest of neighbouring sanguines. Variable as the wind itself, the element of air is strikingly apt for this temperament.

Our fourth principle, the main characteristic of which applies only to ourselves, is that of *self-consciousness*, the possession of an ego or sense of 'I'. This points up one of the main differences between the human kingdom and the animal kingdom: animals are conscious, but we are *self*-conscious. The little word 'I' is unique in that a person may use it of herself or himself, but of no-one else. It is this sense of 'I' or *ego* which represents the factor of individualization, which guarantees the uniqueness of every man, woman and child, and bestows the sense of identity – the consciousness of self. It is the ego that is responsible for co-ordinating the whole of the personality and character of each one of us. It is the principle which allows us, through the faculty of memory, to observe our own actions, benefit from our mistakes, foster our moral development, and so on, from babyhood to old age.

In terms of Ancient Greek science, the element of *fire* is inseparable from anything that is hot, or even warm; and for this reason it is associated with our *blood*. The association of heat with the choleric temperament is clearly evident. Language itself takes up this notion in terms like 'hot-blooded', 'hot-tempered', 'warm-hearted' and suchlike – all characteristics of choleric individuals to a greater or lesser degree. In many respects our ego represents our 'higher self', and ever-striving cholerics, bent always on what they regard as 'self-improvement' in some shape or form, are perpetually prone, with their fiery enthusiasms and consuming passions, to generate heat if not always light. There is usually plenty of hot air to be endured when cholerics are around, particularly when they are warming to their subject.

Of course you love your neighbour

To understand all, as the saying goes, is to forgive all; and most negative feelings vanish in the presence of forgiveness. There is no doubt that a knowledge of the four temperaments is a great help when it comes to tolerating those irritating little habits, seemingly in-grained ways of looking at things, apparently fixed ideas, the "there s/he goes again" kind of reaction we all countenance in our nearest and dearest as well as ordinary friends and acquaintances. We may also with some justification employ the cliché that know-ledge is power, because with increasing knowledge of ourselves and others we do find within ourselves a commensurate ability to control ourselves. This is not to say that we should let everyone walk all over us or allow ourselves to be manipulated in our determination to tolerate insult or injury, or put up with sheer bad behaviour, rudeness, or sheer lack of consideration. It is almost always preferable to wait patiently for the 'psychological moment', for when the time is ripe for maximum impact, before doing the other party the favour of imparting a little 'life-wisdom'. This could range from a punch on the nose to providing a shoulder to cry on, but most of us know – or learn to know – what kind of behaviour is most appropriate, and when.

   It is easy to forget the fact that we actually possess all

four temperaments, but in varying proportions according to our individual constitution. The very word *temperament* itself derives from the Latin word to mix (in due proportion), and this should be borne in mind. If we had equal proportions of all four we would be the most balanced people imaginable, capable of calling into play whatever qualities were needed to equalize matters in any given situation. If we are attending an auction sale, for example, we should need all our wits about us in order to spot potential bargains in the most sanguine of ways; possess enough phlegmatic firmness and self-control in order not to be tempted into paying too much for them; exercise sufficient melancholic resignation when we discover that what we bought was not quite the bargain we had first thought, and adequate choleric resourcefulness to 'improve' it, plus unlimited determination to recoup whatever losses at the next auction sale!

We are all 'God's chil'en', and all cast in the same mould. We are all made of the same stuff, whether physical, psychological, spiritual, mental, physical, emotional, moral – take your pick. This has to be so, otherwise we would never understand one another, and there could be no social interaction. Ordinary social skills necessarily include those of getting on with our fellows; and this is really what this book is about.

All this suggests that the better we know ourselves, our real, deep-down selves that face us every time we look in the mirror, the better. Those lines which appear on our faces after the bloom of youth has faded, and which grow ever longer and deeper as the years go by – it is they which tell of our real selves, for they have been etched there by our own habitual attitudes and behaviour. And it is by learning to know ourselves that we come to learn about one another.

So when, in our daily life, we encounter people of varying mixtures of personal characteristics, we shall be able the more easily to step into their shoes, and to call up sufficient knowledge of the temperaments to know how to treat them in ways that are truly appropriate; that is to say, with genuine care and consideration. In that way we shall be showing forth to them the kind of non-possessive, unconditional, so-called 'Christian' kind of love which has little in common with mere sentiment. Whatever temperament we each possess we are indeed each a member of a 'world family'.

We must never forget that it was truly an act of love between two individuals that brought each one of us into the world, and it is by love we are nurtured. And all know that actions speak louder than words, and it is they that reveal our true motives. It is something of a maxim of psychology that every single action we perform is in response to some need, *whatever that need may be*. It is what we actually *do* that matters, rather than what we say, what we feel, or what we think. If the impulse to perform some deed or other is overwhelming, then it is through this action that we express our true, inner selves. And this, in the last resort, has to be an expression of *love* – of our own selves, for one another, regardless of race, colour, creed – or temperament.

Appendix I – Hints for Dedicated People-Watchers

One of the main assertions made in this book is that our *physiological* and our *psychological* natures are complementary and parallel. The question as to which came first suggests the old chicken-and-egg problem: does our physiognomy or bodily constitution determine our psychological makeup, or vice versa? Here we are faced with the difficult question of spirit and matter, inner and outer, visible and invisible, tangible and intangible, sensory and supersensory. However, I have dropped enough hints along the way to indicate my own firmly held standpoint, which is that *spirit* is at all times and in all circumstances antecedent to *matter*; and it follows from this that we as human beings are primarily spiritual beings, and only secondarily physical-material beings. The outer is a faithful copy of the inner; the manifest of the unmanifest; the material of the spiritual, the creative of the created. Our bodily features do not *form themselves* out of their own resources; the various cells, tissues and so on do not divide and multiply randomly; they *are formed* and organized in accordance with certain definite structural patterns. Biologists will say, yes, of course – what do you think DNA is all about? But I will say, yes, OK – but what formed the DNA which forms...?

Everyone has to make up his or her own mind about all this; but the fact remains that a person of a certain bodily type stands more than an average chance of exhibiting behaviours that are characteristic of that type. Of course there are always those maverick variables and extenuating factors which blur the edges, but nothing is entirely black or white, and people are, after all, capable of modifying and even changing their temperaments, provided that their ego is strong enough. It is all those variables – mixed in due proportion of course – which ensure that we are the same only different. And it is that that makes people so interesting, and people-watching so fascinating. Whilst being acutely aware of the universal characteristics which we all possess in varying degrees, you must always bear in mind that behind these, orchestrating and manipulating them, is that powerful co-ordinating agent – the ego. But the nature of a person's ego can also be determined given the time and opportunity to study the ways in which it operates. The more you are capable of close and accurate observation, and the better you are at attending to those important finer details, the better you will become at assessing people's character from their bodily type and their behaviour. It takes practice, of course, but it is all so very absorbing, so it is impossible to be bored in any company!

"Hail, divinest Melancholy!"
"Hence, loathéd Melancholy!"

It would seem, judging from these contradictory exclamations uttered long ago by the poet John Milton, that he couldn't make up his mind! Melancholy itself is sweet to melancholics only as long as they can enjoy it, wallow in it, luxuriate in it, which they often do. But on the principle that "too much honey spoils the flavour", the time comes when even they desert it – but only to become even more melancholic, for in no way are they likely to "snap out of it". Remember that their inner world is far more important than any outer world, and because people who are possessed of this temperament are invariably complex and often 'difficult', they need very careful handling. Being very private individuals, and often appearing shy and reserved (although they are secretly longing to declaim from the housetops just what wonderful people they are), their strong egotism demands that they be noticed.

In noticing them, look for certain characteristics which may help you.

Very often, they give the impression that their head is too heavy for their body, and they may incline it to one side or other ever so slightly, or perhaps when sitting support their chin in their hands. It is sometimes difficult to decide between the "tall and thin" leptomorphic sanguines and melancholics just as it is the "short and fat" eurymorphic cholerics and phlegmatics. Take especial notice of the length of the face generally, and look for heavy-lidded eyes, a long, thin nose with oval rather than rounded nostrils, thin upper lip, fairly prominent cheekbones and narrowing jaws, with the whole perched on a long neck. These attributes, as well as sloping shoulders, give the impression of burdensome weight, and it is important to remember that it is always an effort for melancholics to drag their bodies about after them. They are usually finely boned and slightly built, and the hands in particular are elegantly formed, and the fingers long and slim. The interesting thing is that the physical body is under direct control of the ego, and hence a powerful connection exists between the two members; it is principally the effort expended by melancholics to exert themselves in terms of bodily exertion that works back on the ego itself, rendering it inordinately strong.

Those curves!

The image of a pink, plump, chubby baby, soft and well-rounded from all angles, is the prototype of most phlegmatics, in terms of both bodily and psychological characteristics. Very much like infants, they are "real softies" for the most part – but watch out if they are crossed or over-wrought! Contrary to all too common belief, they are almost always good-natured and contented, especially when they are well fed. Their often "roly-poly" figures do not arise through too much in the way of dieting, and the old saying, "the way to a man's heart is through his stomach" can be very true, so take up that suggestion to stop at the next pub or service station if you want to keep that phlegmatic partner sweet! So look out for those tell-tale curves: full cheeks and chin(s), stubby nose, full lips, dullish eyes and general air of disinterestedness. Phlegmatics give the overall impression of being lifeless and dull, and lazy into the bargain, and as they find it distracting and even irritating to be disturbed unless strictly necessary, it is perhaps a good thing to wait until they show some spark of initiative, which is generally in glow-plug condition. If you wish to make contact, ask them to tell you their favourite Irish/Jewish/Scottish or whatever joke – but be prepared with one of your own in advance, which will be expected!

That nose!

The noses of sanguine folk come in a greater variety than those of any other temperament. They come in two main types: most common is the short, snub, turned-up or retroussé nose, and the more tip-tilted it is the more certain you may be that your specimen is sanguine. So whenever the nostrils are angled upwards, and the nosetip higher than its base, the same applies, whether the actual nose itself is thin or fleshy. Well-rounded cheeks often accompany these facial features. If the nose is thin, it may well be truly aquiline in shape, but in any case it will show a tendency to be so formed. Take special note if someone's nose is exceptionally large, though not particularly fleshy, for here again you probably have a sanguine. In addition, sanguines usually possess a slender, graceful neck, and the head seems to have a mobility of its own, busily taking in everything in the environment in rapid sweeps.

Those sanguines who have the melancholic as a secondary temperament may certainly give rise to a few doubts; but take a second look at the whole facial conformation, which if oval or heart-shaped signifies a sanguine; but if lean, and 'hatchet' or 'V' shaped and the jaw narrow, you have a melancholic. The hair, too, may also give a clue. If it is fine, and especially light in colour, and curled or waved, even if slightly, suspect a sanguine. Dark, lank, lifeless hair of whatever texture almost certainly indicates melancholic tendencies. In general sanguines have a clear complexion and fine skin, while melancholics are often pallid, with unresponsive facial features.

Wide boys (and girls)

Cholerics, if not always exactly high and handsome, are always wide.

There can be no mistaking them for phlegmatics upon close scrutiny, because they have square rather than rounded shoulders, and short, sometimes very short, necks and ruddy complexion. Their animated manner of speaking and direct eye contact, their quick, purposeful movements, and their general air of self-confidence contrast strongly with the gentle, amiable, unprepossessing ways and manner of phlegmatics. They can in no way be confused with either pronounced sanguines or melancholics, but some difficulties may arise when the secondary temperament tends towards either of these, especially when people are older. That "middle-aged spread" can easily mask a sanguine, and a corpulent choleric may well be confused with a portly phlegmatic. So the matter of distinguishing between the somatotypes is, as ever, a matter of close study; but the more you practice it the easier it will become.

Make use of your temperament(s)!

As I have stated elsewhere, we possess all four temperaments, just as surely as we are creatures of Fire (blood heat), Air (lung functions), Water (body fluids) and Earth (bones), and as all these elements representing the temperaments are present in us, and all nicely integrated. In physiological terms they are all fairly well balanced out – or should be. If they are not, the resulting maladjustments manifest themselves as illness. Normally, they are beyond our conscious control. As far as our mental and emotional characteristics are concerned, we would like to imagine that we are able to exercize some degree of control over them, even if it is only to a limited extent. It would not be an exaggeration to say that *true self-control lies in the ability to exploit our temperament, consciously and deliberately.* In other words, we would all like to manipulate our temperamental characteristics and propensities to optimal purpose and maximal effect. This, given time and practice, is indeed capable of achievement, even though it would probably take several lifetimes!

However, some idea as to how this can be achieved may be gathered from working on and extending those opportunities to do so when they occur. Although we each possess a main temperament and a secondary one which effectively "smother" or suppress the other two, the less exertive temperamental characteristics are nevertheless present. Just imagine: if we possessed only one temperament, what monstrously one-sided personalities we would be! A pure choleric, unalloyed by the other temperaments, would eventually degenerate into a raging maniac; similarly, a sanguine would become the scattiest of lunatics; a phlegmatic would descend into apathy and imbecility, and a melancholic would regress through unrelievable depression to melancholia proper.

Fortunately, however, ordinary everyday life provides us with plenty of opportunities for keeping ourselves in balance, and this by stimulating universal or 'stock' responses to various situations and circumstances. If there is the lawn to be mown, the sitting room to be wallpapered, or spring-cleaning to be done, we need to call up our choleric propensities and get on with the job, energetically and cheerfully. We are at our most phlegmatic when we wake up in the morning, especially if there is frost and snow outside, or it is blowing a gale! We just do not want to be bothered, for we are far too warm and snug in bed; warm, cosy and comfortable; but duty calls, and so, with a stretch and a yawn... We are in our most sanguine of moods whilst on holiday, when there is variety in plenty, the time to indulge, and to be wonderfully free to do so. And when it comes to Christmas shopping, and we feel justified in splashing out, organizing parties and so on – well! We are all melancholic when misfortune or disaster strikes, when jobs are lost or careers ruined, or a close relative is at death's door. Then everyone tends to become melancholic with us, showering us with sympathy and condolences.

Scenarios such as these are easily imagined, simply because the appropriate thoughts and feelings spring up of themselves. We simply "go along with" the situation, reacting as everyone else almost certainly would – in stock fashion, according to habit or convention. The difficulty of consciously balancing out our inborn qualities and attributes lies in the ability consciously to call up compensating traits and characteristics which we have but which remain dormant or unexercized. So, with diligence and practice we can become, in a manner of speaking, masters of our main temperament rather than its slave, and more rounded personalities as a result. We should at the same time become subject to much less in the way of stress and strain, tension and anxiety, in countless situations which would normally give rise to these undesirable and disturbing states. Above all, we should be happier and healthier right into old age – and who does not wish to be that?

Appendix II – The Riddle of the Four Body Types

In Chapter 2 I discussed the enigma concerning the four temperaments of tradition[1] and the modern scientific notion of the three so-called *somatotypes* or types of body build. Clearly, four into three will not go, so in this chapter – which is aimed at the reader wishing to pursue the matter further and more deeply – I am making the attempt at a solution to the riddle.

The human embryo and its development

The hypothesis of the three physiological types, namely ectomorphic, mesomorphic and endomorphic, (see below) as being determined by their relationship to the three layers of the human embryonic disc is commonly accepted. In terms of biology this disc, also called the blastodisc, is the layer of cells derived from the inner cell mass of the blastocyst, which in turn have originated from the fertilized egg, and from which the embryo develops. The component layers of this disc are called the *ectoderm*, which, after the disc has folded, comprises the outer layer of cells, the *mesoderm*, which constitutes the middle layer, and the *endoderm*, which consists of the inner layer. Based on this scheme of things, physiologists posit the hypothesis of the three somatotypes, which arise, as generally supposed and accepted, from some kind of developmental balance in favour of one of these layers at the expense of the other two. This being so, the somatotypes are posited as resulting from what amounts to an exaggerated deviation from some 'ideal norm' which represents the *perfect* human body. Needless to say, such perfection has rarely, if ever, been found!

These three somatotypes are generally described in terms approximating to the following:

Ectomorph
A lean, muscular human build with a large surface of skin in relation to body weight.
Mesomorph
Characterized by a powerful musculature and a predominantly bony framework.
Endomorph
Physiological type having a relatively fat body with prominent abdominal parts and weak muscular and skeletal development.

The three germ layers (that is to say, the layers of small cells capable of developing into an organism with its parts), comprise the ectoderm, mesoderm and endoderm already mentioned, which arise from the inner cell mass, give rise to all the tissues and organs of the embryo, and eventually, of course, the foetus, child, and then the adult. However, it is important to realise that *the specificity of the germ layers is not rigidly fixed*. In other words, the particular parts of which the mature organism will eventually consist are *not* strictly pre-determined; and this fact is not sufficiently taken into account by the more rigid upholders of the so-called Hypothesis of Embryonic Development, which has existed in various forms since the early nineteenth century until recent times. However, it is now known that the cells of each germ layer divide, migrate, aggregate and differentiate in rather precise patterns as they form the various systems of organs.[2] Division of the early embryo into three primary germ layers is therefore to some extent one of descriptive convenience.[3]

This information in itself is somewhat contradictory in that (a) the three somatotypes are traditionally traceable back to the three embryonic layers as largely a matter of *fact*, but (b) the authors of both books which contain these statements agree that "the specificity of the germ layers is not rigidly fixed" and that these divisions are for "descriptive convenience" rather than for any other reason. However, there is substantial evidence to support the long-held notion that the three layers of the embryonic disc actually do, *in the main*, develop into three main vital systems which secure and maintain the human organism. These will be discussed in some detail later, and are: (1) the ectoderm (brain, and central nervous system, and sense organs, skin, hair); (2) the mesoderm (the vital organs, e.g. heart and lungs, contained mainly within the chest between the neck and the diaphragm, and the vascular system), and (3) the endoderm (the digestive system and other abdominal organs). What may be regarded as a fourth source of body tissues is the mesenchyme, which is a loosely organized fibrous tissue of the mesoderm which gives rise for the most part to the blood, bone, muscles and connective tissues.

Historical aspects of the somatotype theory

It is obvious to all of us from ordinary observation that there are only *two* basic body types, namely the tall and slim, and the short and stocky. This general notion has been apparent for a very long time indeed, for it corresponds respectively to the *Habitus phthisicus* and *Habitus apoplecticus* of Hippocrates (460?-?377BC), the Greek physician well-known as the "father of medicine". In his book *The Structure of Human Personality*, Professor Hans

Eysenck, a former professor of psychology in the University of London, gives many interesting details concerning the whole theory of somatotypes, and it is recommended to those readers sufficiently interested in the somatotype riddle.

The commonsense classification of human body build into short and thickset and tall and slender (eurymorphic and leptomorphic respectively), did not seem to be sufficient for certain natural philosophers of the nineteenth century. They set about seeking a third, intermediary type which would fit neatly between these two relative extremes, and came up with the *mesomorphic* (Greek – middle form) type of person. It seems that they were determined to make the facts fit the theory instead of the other way round – a temptation to many scientists that has sometimes seemed difficult to resist. Thus, such a threefold classification would neatly match the three layers of the embryonic disc, the one-sided development of one of which would then result in one or other of the three bodily types or somatotypes, as follows:

Embryonic disc layer	*Somatotype*	*Body build (approx.)*
endoderm (inner skin)	endomorphic	('short and fat')
mesoderm (middle skin)	mesomorphic	('middle build')
ectoderm (outer skin)	ectomorphic	('tall and thin')

Many nineteenth and early twentieth century scientists were interested in determining correlations between the embryonic disc layers and consequent physical structure and conformation, but the jaw-cracking terms they invented need not concern us. The terms that have survived and are in common use are those applied by the British researcher W H Sheldon, and I have employed these throughout.

However, all the energy and ingenuity expended by the many psychologists, psychiatrists and others in their attempts to match up the three embryonic layers with the three body types of ordinary observation, namely those appearing in the table above, appears to have been useless endeavour. Their persistent aspirations seem to have been dashed by recent research into embryology, as I have already indicated by the earlier quotations from the books by Moore, and Beck and Moffat. The mathematical ruling that four temperaments will not 'go' into three somatotypes is therefore seen to be absolute. In other words, earlier theories are rendered insupportable, and the search for a valid solution must be sought elsewhere.

A solution to the problem

Among the many researchers was the French scientist Martigny, who in the late forties of the twentieth century posited the actuality of a fourth body type, to which he gave the term *chordoblastic*, of which more later. This, according to him, was that somatotype most closely in accord with what most other researchers have called the *mesomorphic*. By reason of Martigny's hypothesis an element of confusion was introduced, and I will do my best to clarify the issues involved. The following table indicates the correspondence between the body types that he posited:

Martigny's terms	*Body build (after Martigny)*
mesoblastique (mesomorphic)	muscular, athletic
chordoblastique	normal, balanced
entoblastique (endomorphic)	abdominal
ectoblastique (ectomorphic)	leptosomatic ('tall & thin')

You will see that his term 'chordoblastic' refers to the 'middle' or normal, balanced type of bodily constitution and structure, and this is important for arriving at a satisfactory solution to this whole question.

Now, in the stereotypical outlines of physical appearance according to temperament, which appear at Figure 2 on p. 21, correspondences make themselves evident.

After Martigny	After Sheldon	After temperament
mesoblastique	mesomorphic	choleric
chordoblastique	–	sanguine
entoblastique	endomorphic	phlegmatic
ectoblastique	ectomorphic	melancholic

Now it is easy to see where the gaps in the tables occur, and where part – but only part – of the confusion arises. Martigny, in his classification, prefers to employ the scientific term derived from *blastos* (Greek for *bud* or *shoot*) in referring to embryonic development, eg 'mesoblastique, ectoblastique'. This describes the layers of cells which, in the earliest stage of embryonic development, is not much thicker than skin, hence the terms ending in '*-derm*', which is derived from the Greek word *derma* (skin). This term is often applied to 'skin' or 'layer of cells', so for all practical purposes the words used by Martigny and those by Sheldon are identical in meaning and application.

However, confusion is piled on confusion in that Sheldon persisted in referring to the 'digestive type', namely the *endomorphics*, whose build is associated with "a relatively fat body with prominent abdominal parts" – obviously our fat and jolly *phlegmatics*. The *ectomorphics* Sheldon associates with the skin itself, together with the sense organs, nervous system and brain – quite obviously the "lean muscular build with a large area of surface skin in relation to body weight" which identifies those of *melancholic* temperament. This leaves us with those whose physical build comes between these two extreme types, namely the *mesomorphic* physique, and this is indicative of the *sanguine* temperament. Now, our three generally accepted somatotypes – endomorphs, mesomorphs and ectomorphs – have been reasonably successfully matched to phlegmatics, sanguines and melancholics respectively.

This leaves no room for the *choleric* temperament – the hard-muscled, square-shouldered, short and stocky type of person. As you can see from the above Table, the choleric physique is identified, in the judgement of Sheldon at least, together with the phlegmatic physique as *endomorphic*. Here, then, we have confusion concerning the 'short and fat' category, for at first glance, and without reasonable study of their characteristics in appearance and general behaviour, it can be difficult to distinguish between the two. At closer examination, of course, such differentiation is relatively easily made.

So much for confusion on the part of Sheldon. At this point, if you are not tearing your hair, or abandoned my sincere and earnest attempts to clarify matters – or both – I beg your indulgence as to the contribution of Martigny. As can be seen from Figure 3, he correctly divines that there are indeed four somatotypes, which should, according to the criteria I have adopted, fit the four temperaments with glove-like perfection. But do they? Well, er – yes. That is – I mean to say – *almost*.

The problem is that he has, like Sheldon, confused the two endomorphic types of physique, and made the same – to my mind, at least – incorrect judgements. However, Martigny designated the muscular, square-shouldered model as *mesomorphic* in build and stature, namely the 'middle' or balanced, harmonious build which I have typified as belonging to the *sanguine* temperament. This we can clearly see

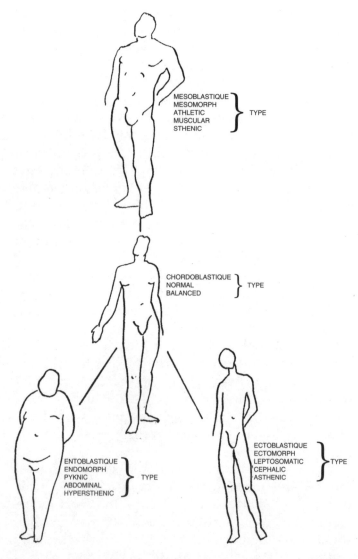

Figure 3: Martigny's diagrammatic representation of the three Main Body Types derived according to the Hypothesis of Embryological Development.

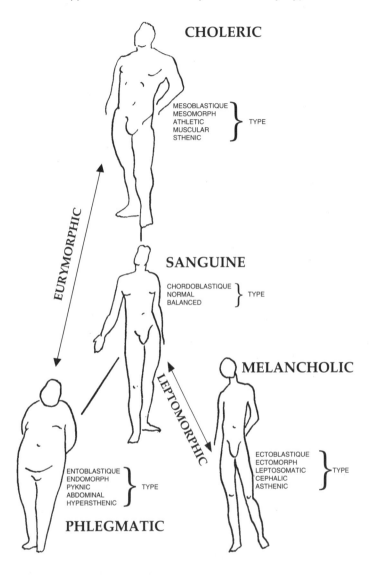

Figure 4: The author's adaptation of Martigny's illustration on the facing page.

from his characterizations in Figure 3. He has clearly identified and stereotyped the *ectomorphic* physique with melancholic, 'cephalic' or 'head' person, the typical introvert.

Now, what we have identified as being the sanguine body type, Martigny has indicated as *chordoblastique* (Greek – *chorde*, string [of gut], *blastos*, bud, shoot). This is a term not employed by Sheldon and most other writers on the subject, for reasons best known to them. However, it is probable, or even certain, that Martigny, from his evident knowledge of embryology, took good notice of the fact that the cells of the embryonic spinal chord, to which the term refers, eventually develop from the neural crest cells, derived from the *neuroectoderm*. These cells develop into spinal, cranial, and autonomic ganglia, ensheathing cells of the peripheral nervous system, and the coverings of the brain and spinal chord, as well as muscle connective tissues, among other functions. Thus we have the two somatotypes connected with the *ectodermal layer* of the embryonic disc accounted for, namely the sanguine and melancholic, and the two connected with the *endodermal layer*, namely the choleric and phlegmatic. All this is perfectly reasonable, for here we have our two basic types of physical build – the tall and slender and the short and thickset respectively.

But this is not the end of the story, for there is the missing link to account for – and that is the *mesodermal layer*.

Now by definition, the mesodermal layer is the *middle* layer of cells which, in the embryonic disc, must of course lie sandwiched between the ectoderm and the endoderm, as in the following sketch:

Figure 5

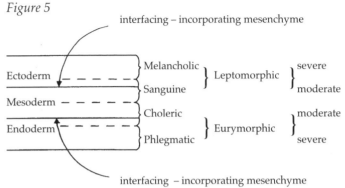

Now, the interesting thing is this: the two surfaces (call them the upper and lower for the sake of convenience) of the mesodermal layer *must interface with the other two layers,* namely the endoderm on one side and the ectoderm on the other. I venture to suggest that the ectodermal layer does indeed give rise to the *two* leptomorphic (tall and thin) types, both originating in the *ectoderm,* namely the melancholic (extreme) and the sanguine (moderate) temperament physiognomies, and the *two* eurymorphic (short and heavily built) types, both originating in the *endoderm,* namely the phlegmatic (extreme) and the choleric (moderate) physiognomies. Furthermore, I suggest that the two 'middle' somatotypes, namely the moderate leptomorph (sanguine temperament) and the moderate eurymorph (choleric temperament) obtain their 'moderating' influences from the event of their being interfaced with the *mesoderm,* one on either of the two surfaces. We have seen earlier that no hard and fast rules can be laid down concerning the eventual 'destinations' of the embryonic cells in terms of bodily organs and connective tissues and covering; only the main categories of these are constant with regard to their ultimate functional destination.

Thus we arrive at a possible solution to the riddle,

and in this the Table on the facing page will help to clarify the whole situation:

The principle of threefolding extended

As we have seen quite clearly, the basically threefold nature of the embryonic disc, which in turn prompted the early researchers to seek for correspondences in terms of human bodily structure and conformation, is of considerable significance. What is of equal significance is that our whole bodily constitution can, as I have already mentioned on p. 125, be divided also into three general categories: (1) our system encompassing our network of sense organs, with its complementary scheme of brain and nervous system; (2) our chest organization, enveloping our rhythmic system, namely our heart and lungs, and (3) our digestive or metabolic system. For present practical purposes our limbs may be regarded somewhat in the nature of peripheral appendages – undeniably important in their general functions, but not of vital consequence, as no life-supporting organs are involved.

These three systems can with some justification be seen as reflecting this threefold principle, for the origins of these vital systems are the three layers of the embryonic disc. It goes without saying that any kind of strict compartmentalizing with respect to the 'systems' outlined below is not envisaged as part of any model that I posit. The skin and sensory nervous system is spread over and throughout the body; the cardio-vascular system, with the heart as vital organ also extends to the whole body, which serves, and is served by, the digestive system and its ancillary organs. Every system, and every component organ

Composite Table of Attributes

Factor	Phlegmatic	Choleric	Sanguine	Melancholic
Origin	Endoderm	Mesoderm	Mesoderm	Ectoderm
Physique	Eurymorphic	Eurymorphic	Leptomorphic	Leptomorphic
Somatotype	Endomorphic (severe)	Endomorphic (moderate)	Ectomorphic (moderate)	Ectomorphic (severe)
Orientation	Introverted	Extraverted	Extraverted	Introverted
Thinking	Convergent	Divergent	Divergent	Convergent
Balance	Stable	Unstable	Stable	Unstable
Attitude to time	Present (bodily state)	Future (outer events)	Present (mental state)	Past (inner state)
Directional tendencies	Centripetal (systolic)	Centrifugal (diastolic)	Centrifugal (diastolic)	Centripetal (systolic)
Difficulties	Personal	Behavioural	Behavioural	Personal
Basic social attitude	Antipathetic	Sympathetic	Sympathetic	Antipathetic

of every system, is totally dependent on the efficient functioning of the rest. These systems eventually become incorporated in the human constitution in corresponding fashion, as follows:

Ectoderm
(head system):   gives rise to the skin and nails, the central nervous system (brain and spinal chord) the peripheral nervous system, sensory epithelia of the ears, eyes and nose, among other organs.

Mesoderm
(chest system):   gives rise to the heart, blood and lymph vessels and cells, membranes lining the heart, lungs and peritoneum, and other organs, including kidneys, spleen, ovaries and testes.

Endoderm
(digestive system)   gives rise to the epithelial linings of the gastro-intestinal and respiratory tracts, bladder, etc., and the essential tissues of the liver, pancreas and various glands.

This is merely a sketch, but the correlationship between the three layers of the embryonic disc and the three main systems of vital organs is clearly discernible. Bearing in mind the fact that the 'destinations' reached in terms of actual bodily organs are only loosely determined, this leaves room for considerable latitude, scope or even liberty for development from embryo to mature human being. The parallels are too close to be ignored, and I offer these observations as food for thought among those readers sufficiently interested to have followed me so far.

A further extension of the model

The problem of trying to make four go into three may be an arithmetical impossibility, but it is possible in terms of the human constitution, thanks to a certain flexibility on the part of Nature! Just as the four temperaments cannot be said to be rigidly compartmentalized, so it is with the 'straying' cells during embryonic development. This continuous process of cell division and migration eventually forms the physical-material basis for our senses by which we become aware of the world. Our organization of brain and nervous system which supports it, and the mental processes facilitated by this, allows us to *experience consciousness* and to reflect on our experiences, both outer and inner.

Our life of *cognition* (thinking), *affect* (feeling) and *willing* (impulse to purposeful action) associated with our mental processes in their broadest application, is also not rigidly compartmentalized, as we know from everyday experience. What we *do*, or what we determine in full consciousness, which in the last analysis is what matters, is almost entirely dependent on what we *feel* and / or what we *think*. Any organization, including of course the human constitution as a functioning whole, must be entirely interdependent, and so boundaries between the manifold operations are more apparent than real, as has been maintained all along. Similarly, there are no boundaries between our four temperaments, which are blended 'in due proportion' to make up our characteristics, and help to make us what we are as individuals. The entire *system of systems* is seen to complement one another, resulting in an organization that is matchless in its elegant efficacy and efficiency.

As we have already determined, the melancholic temperament is the polar opposite to the phlegmatic. Interestingly enough, melancholics are mainly concerned with their inner world of thinking, and may be thought of as being 'head types'. They are *convergent* in their thinking habits as well as being *introverted*, concerned with their own problems. Opposing the melancholic temperament is the phlegmatic, which, as we have seen, is closely associated with the digestive system, so that they may with justification be designated as 'metabolic types'. We also know that the *ectoderm* of the embryonic disc is mainly associated in maturational and organizational terms with the head and central nervous system, and this is precisely the field of operations, so to speak, of those whose main temperament is melancholic. (See Figures 5 and 6)

Now, the *endoderm* of the embryonic disc gives rise mainly to the digestive or metabolic system, which is situated at the locality which is furthest away, namely in the lower regions of the abdomen. I have contended

Figure 6

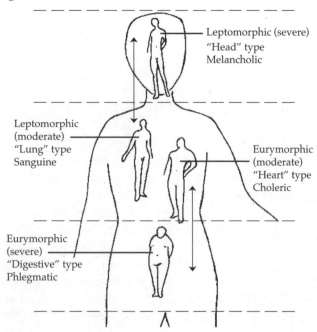

Leptomorphic (severe)
"Head" type
Melancholic

Leptomorphic
(moderate)
"Lung" type
Sanguine

Eurymorphic
(moderate)
"Heart" type
Choleric

Eurymorphic
(severe)
"Digestive" type
Phlegmatic

Figure 7

Melancholic
Severe Leptomorph
Unstable
Convergent
Introvert (reflective)
Personal difficulties

Sanguine
Moderate Leptomorph
Stable
Divergent
Extrovert (active)
Behavioural difficulties

Choleric
Moderate Eurymorph
Unstable
Divergent
Extrovert (active)
Behavioural difficulties

Phlegmatic
Severe Eurymorph
Stable
Convergent
Introvert (reflective)
Personal difficulties

earlier that the melancholic 'cerebral' types are polarically opposed to the 'digestive' types; and this they certainly are in the senses of location and function. Furthermore, we are *conscious* and aware in our brain and central nervous system, but almost totally *unconscious* in our digestive processes. If we do become conscious of them, then something has to be wrong somewhere!

But, as well as being polar opposites in many ways, they also have significant similarities. People of both these temperaments are introverted in their basic orientation and convergent in their mental processes. In the case of phlegmatics, however, their 'normal' consciousness is, as it were, dimmed by reason of their preoccupation with their digestions! They are, as we have seen, the slowest, most sluggish, and most unaware in terms of *outer* sense-impressions, compared with people of any other temperament. Conversely, their consciousness is keener where their *inner*, metabolic processes are involved. Upon reflection, all these factors can be seen to tie in quite neatly in terms of my hypothesis.

Between the ectoderm on the one hand, and the endoderm on the other lies, by very definition, the *mesoderm*, which incorporates the *mesenchyme*. (See Figure 5, p. 133) This, also as we have seen, gives rise to the heart, blood and lymph vessels and cells, and for the most part the lungs and other thoracic organs, with most of their connective tissues arising from the mesenchyme, to which is traceable bone and cartilage, blood, and connective tissues. Now, I have posited that the head forms the main region of operations for those of mainly melancholic propensities, and the digestive organs for those of phlegmatic disposition. Being faced with the problem of determining the 'locations' in terms of function of these two types, I have little choice but to argue that the two other temperaments must be connected with organs to be found in the human thorax, and this is what I now contend.

The main vital organs located in the chest, and both serving the body in significantly complementary ways, are of course the *heart* and the *lungs*. The heart brings about the circulation of the blood by means of its supporting system of arteries and veins, and is the carrier of oxygen to all parts of our body. In addition, its functions include the transportation to all bodily organs of vital nutritive substances which, I scarcely need add, are made available by the digestive system and its proc- esses. Hence, we have an 'air' organism in the shape of the lungs and their function, and a 'heat' organization provided, by means of the blood and its action, by the 'combustive' processes of the digestive system. I con- tend therefore that the *sanguine* temperament is associated with the *lungs*, and the choleric with the *blood*. (See also Figures 2 and 6)

Further support may be gained from the observa- tion that sanguines, with their flighty, nervous, fidgety ways, and their well-known bird-like talent of not missing anything that goes on around them, are evi- dently connected with the nervous system, particularly those parts of it which serve the sense-organs. It is therefore reasonable to contend that sanguine people have tendencies which betray the fact that their tem- peramental qualities and attributes are allied to those organs which owe their origins to its close physical proximity to the *ectoderm*, (responsible for the future development of the brain, nervous system, etc) with which it interfaces or interconnects.

Moreover, this similarity is complemented, as in the case of the ectoderm/head system and the endoderm/ digestive system, also by their very polarities. That is to say, the mesoderm interfaces with the *endoderm* just as it does with the ectoderm, and this being so, deductive reasoning suggests the inference that the *choleric* temperament should find certain connections with the *digestive system*, and I insist that this is so. Whereas cholerics are extroverted in their behaviour and divergent in their thinking, they manifest the ob- verse of the phlegmatics, who are introverted in their general attitudes and behaviour and convergent in their thinking. It will be recalled that sanguines are also, like the cholerics, extroverted in their behaviour and divergent in their thinking. Observation and argument along the lines I have indicated therefore reveals an elegantly balanced model of how neatly our physical and mental organizations complement each other.

Just as the pattern is, as it were, set by the three layers of the embryonic disc, so these three layers are represented in horizontal fashion by a fully developed human being who is standing in vertical pose. Comparing my sketches (Figures 3 and 4) may be helpful in grasping my arguments and contentions.

The upper layer, encompassing the head and neck, represents the ectoderm, irrespective of the fact that the network of the central nervous system extends to all other parts of the body.

This, according to my model, represents the organs which have to the greatest degree derived from the embryonic ectoderm, and gives emphasis to those which in particular form the physical basis for the melancholic temperament to develop. The uppermost stratum of the central layer or mesoderm, which in the sketch is seen to interface with the ectoderm's upper surface, is represented in the region of the upper chest, taking in most of the lungs, and including the region of the heart. This area, if developed somewhat advantageously in relation to the other parts of the body, thereby imparts the appropriate conditions to facilitate the establishing of the sanguine temperament.

By means of overlapping, the lower stratum of the mesoderm also takes in this region, which then extends downwards so that its lower surface interfaces with the upper surface of the endoderm. This area represents the corresponding strata of the 'lower' part of the endoderm, and, if over-developed at the expense of the other cellular layers, evolves in such a way as to confer such facilities as will allow the emergence of choleric attitudes and behaviour in the fully developed person.

Finally, the lower layer, or endoderm, can be seen to take in the whole of the abdomen, and includes the whole region that allows of all our digestive / metabolic organization. This is the main region of concern for most phlegmatics for much of the time, and may fully be understood to represent the basis of the phlegmatic temperament. In substantiation of this, Figure 5 will be found to be helpful.

This simple table may assist in clarifying issues further:

Temperament	Body build	Orientation	Cognitive type	Physique
Melancholic	Ectomorphic (severe)	Introverted	Convergent	Leptomorphic
Sanguine	Ectomorphic (moderate)	Extroverted	Divergent	Leptomorphic
Choleric	Endomorphic (moderate)	Extroverted	Divergent	Eurymorphic
Phlegmatic	Endomorphic (severe)	Introverted	Convergent	Eurymorphic

From this table – and Figures 5 and 7 – you will see that I have not included the so-called *mesomorphic* somatotype – *simply because there isn't one*! It is an invention of those who wished slavishly to maintain the false notion that there is some kind of 'middle build'. In reality there are only *two* types of physique, and these are the *leptomorphic* (tall and slender), and the *eurymorphic* (short and stocky) categories of common observation. The so-called mesomorphic type is represented by a moderate build of leptomorph resulting in a shorter, more balanced and harmonious body build characteristic of most sanguines, and the equally moderate physique, rather less gross and heavy than the extreme, of the eurymorphic type, representing the choleric physiognomy.

Looked at in the ways that I have, it seems perfectly reasonable to claim that four temperaments 'go into' *four* somatotypes, and not three – for there are in reality only *two* somatotypes: *one severe and one moderate of each type*. Furthermore, my ordering of the human body into head organization, lung and heart organization, and digestive organization fits this hypothesis perfectly. These three organ systems correspond reasonably well with the original conception of three embryonic cell layers, allowing for the non-specific nature of normal cell division during the embryonic stages of development which allows for mutations, migrations, aggregations and suchlike.

Some nineteenth century scientists suspected that there was something not quite right about the four temperaments 'going' into three somatotypes, speculating that either the mesenchyme of the mesoderm, or the interfacing surfaces themselves had some part in it all, and I contend that in this I have been able to vindicate them in considerable measure.

References

(1)   Steiner R – *The Four Temperaments*, Rudolf Steiner Publishing Co, 1944, p. 6; Childs, G J – *Steiner Education in Theory and Practice*, Floris Books, 1991, Chapter 6.

(2)   Moore K L – *The Developing Human*, W B Saunders Co, 1988, 4th edition, p 69.

(3)   Beck F and Moffat D B – *Human Embryology and Genetics*, Blackwell Scientific Publications, 1973, p 128.

Steiner Education and Social Issues, How Waldorf Schooling Addresses the Problems of Society
Brien Masters

Time for Transformation, Through Darkness to the Light
Margarete van den Brink and Hans Stolp

Under the Sky, Playing, Working and Enjoying Adventures in the Open Air
Sally Schweizer

Well I Wonder..., Childhood in the Modern World, A Handbook for Parents, Carers and Teachers
Sally Schweizer

A Woman's Path, Motherhood, Love and Personal Development
Almut Bockemühl

Your Reincarnating Child, Welcoming a Soul to the World
Gilbert Childs and Sylvia Childs